THE
LISKEARD AND LOOE
BRANCH

Looe station, looking south from the platform on 28th June 1948.

R. K. Cope

THE
LISKEARD AND LOOE
BRANCH

GERRY BEALE

WILD SWAN PUBLICATIONS LTD.

For Renate, Tom and Alice
who live with and tolerate my obsession

Looking east from the beach at Looe c.1950. *J. H. Moss*

ACKNOWLEDGEMENTS

As with any work of this nature, many people have had a hand in its creation and without their help and encouragement this book would never have seen the light of day. Thanks must go firstly to my parents for deciding that the family holiday in 1966 should be spent in Cornwall, thus allowing me to make the acquaintance of the Liskeard and Looe branch for the first time. We drove into Looe for a day trip but I was able to travel by train back to Liskeard where I was collected — a journey which allowed me to experience the beauty of the East Looe River valley for the first time and, moreover, when much of the steam era infrastructure was still in place.

The contribution of former railwaymen Keith Trembeth and Larry Crozier has already been recorded in my introduction, but I was also able to talk to Joe Trethewey, former shedmaster at Oxford locomotive shed who, as the son of a china clay worker from Roche, started his railway career as an engine cleaner at St. Blazey in the 1930s. These people's contributions brought to life some of the incidents recorded in the photographs and enabled me to interpret some events which I would otherwise have been unable to do.

It should be apparent from the illustrations in this book that the Liskeard and Looe branch is well recorded in photographs. This is no doubt a result of its fascinating history — a number of articles on the line appeared in the pages of the *Railway Magazine* over the years which meant that railway enthusiasts were well aware of it — and of its location in a popular holiday area. It seems that any railway enthusiast worth his salt would take time out from the Cornish family holiday to visit the line and duly record it on film. One of the difficulties in putting together this book was making the picture selection from the wealth of material available — often it was a case of what to leave out rather than what to include. Wherever possible, I have tried to credit the photographers individually with their work, but this has not always been possible, so if anyone recognises an uncredited picture, I can only apologise in advance for the omission. All the photographers that I contacted for prints of their negatives were, without exception, most helpful in supplying me with the prints I required. I would also like to thank Roger Carpenter for bearing my interests in mind through the years — from time to time an envelope would drop through the door and inside would be a few more views of the Looe branch.

In a similar vein I would like to thank Chris Turner who, whilst undertaking his own researches, kept my interests in mind and kept up a steady flow of information, much of it from official sources. The majority of it was of great use but I have to say that some was what might be termed minutiae — if you need to know when additional electric lighting was added to the gentlemen's lavatory at Looe station, I can tell you! Chris's contribution has added a great deal to the official records held at the Public Record Office where the staff were as helpful as they always are. Thanks should also go to Adrian Gray for his work on the GWR locomotive allocation registers held at Kew, again work which was undertaken on my behalf while other subjects were being pursued.

Thanks are also due, in no small measure, to Robert Tivendale for allowing me to have access to the documents, photographs and other material from the Norman Burrows collection which is now in his care. I'm sure that Robert thought the day would never come when this book would appear in print, but now that it has, I am only too pleased to be able to thank him for his assistance.

A special thank you is due to Malcolm and Mandy Mitchell for their kindness and generous hospitality over the years when I was making the numerous trips to Cornwall that were necessary to complete this work.

A special debt of thanks is also due to Paul Karau for his constant enthusiasm and encouragement in this and other projects. Just as he has so many times before, Paul has worked his magic with the material presented to him and made the book into what I hoped it would be — an attractive tribute to a most appealing and interesting piece of railway.

Finally, thanks are due to Renate for her help and encouragement. She had to endure the piles of papers and other documents spread all over the dining room for months on end while the main text was being written and she has accompanied me on trips to Looe, or up onto the moors, when visiting Cornwall in search of the inspiration necessary to see the work to completion.

ISBN 1 874103 47 X

Designed by Paul Karau
Printed by Amadeus Press Ltd., Cleckheaton

Published by
WILD SWAN PUBLICATIONS LTD.
1-3 Hagbourne Road, Didcot, Oxon, OX11 8DP

CONTENTS

Leaving Liskeard for Looe.   *J. L. Rapson*

No. 4584 on a down train nearing Looe on 26th May 1957. On this most scenic section of the line, from Sandplace to the terminus, the railway surely belongs to the landscape as much as the East Looe River itself.

R. J. Sellick

INTRODUCTION

As I write, it has just started snowing again. The view through my window is of white encrusted trees and shrubs in the garden, whilst indoors the central heating is working overtime to keep the chill air at bay. It is about as great a contrast as possible to my own personal Cornish idyll — an early summer's day, perhaps May or June, in the East Looe river valley. In my imagination I am beside the Liskeard and Looe branch, about a mile and a half from the coastal terminus, perhaps walking along the road where it parallels the railway track. Here, next to the river, the line runs along a low embankment and is separated from the neighbouring road by a fence of post-and-wire. Almost the only sound to be heard, apart from the occasional passing road vehicle, is the water rippling against the bank, whilst out in the middle of the river, waterfowl are to be seen bobbing up and down as they rest on the water's surface. As the level of the river is gently raised by the incoming tide, luxuriously foliated trees overhang the opposite bank, the boughs almost touching the water, and the reeded flats further upstream of this tidal water make a scene of great beauty and tranquillity.

Eventually the calm is disturbed by the shriek of an engine whistle echoing along the valley. A down passenger train is on its way and is warning the Terras level crossing keeper of its approach. Soon the characteristic sounds of a free-wheeling Great Western locomotive become apparent as the engine rounds the sharp bend in the track. The 45XX 2—6—2T bustles past with its vacuum pump 'spitting' and its train of three carriages snaking obediently behind, packed to capacity with trippers. Children's eager faces at the open windows, perhaps enthralled by the beauty of the passing scenery, are barely able to contain their excitement at the prospect of a day by the seaside. Rounding the next sharp bend, the engine whistles again before the train disappears from view almost as suddenly as it appeared. Peace returns to the valley and the waterfowl, out in the middle of the river, continue quite unconcernedly floating up and down on the water's surface.

Sadly, this scene can only be a creation of my imagination for I never experienced the Liskeard and Looe branch when steam operation of the line was the rule. I visited the area for the first time in 1966 when a two-car diesel unit worked the passenger service. The goods service had also finished but otherwise the branch remained as fascinating as it had always been. The curious branch station at Liskeard situated at a right-angle to the main line, still in 1966 with the noticeboards permitting certain classes of steam locomotive onto the branch, the unusual reversal at Coombe Junction, the intimate nature of the valley scenery giving way to the wider riverscapes as the train made its way down the branch and, finally, the half-buried

rails on the quay at Looe, all made an indelible impression on my mind and instilled a fascination with the line which has remained with me ever since. The compilation of this book is the result of several years research, collecting photographs, plans, etc, in an attempt to understand how the line looked and worked before the rationalisation of the Beeching era.

One of the pleasures of the research work has been the opportunity of meeting and talking with railwaymen, all now retired, who worked the steam services on the branch in the 1940s and '50s. Former signalman Larry Crozier and fireman Keith Trembeth both made me welcome in their homes and patiently responded to my many questions. Their answers enabled me to build up a picture of how the line was operated in the latter years of steam and brought to life many of the instances recorded in the photographs reproduced here. In addition, their comments made me realize what a self-contained operation the branch was, a result, possibly, of its history as an independent minor

Looking up the river to Terras level crossing in 1961.   *G. Tilt*

1

railway and its late connection with the remainder of Britain's railway system. There was no through running between the branch and the main line, whilst the Motive Power Department at Moorswater always felt itself to be isolated from the parent depot only a few miles away at St. Blazey.

It is the intention of this work to portray the line as it was under GWR and British Railways ownership. Other writers have chronicled the earlier history of the independent railway, and its canal predecessor, most notably Michael J. Messenger in *Caradon and Looe: The Canal, Railways and Mines* published by Twelveheads Press in 1978. Sadly, this book is currently out of print but I must acknowledge the kindness of the author in permitting me to extract information from it. For those who require further details of the earlier history of the Liskeard and Looe and Liskeard and Caradon Railways, I can do no better than to recommend Michael Messenger's work and hope that the title will soon appear in print again.

Before finalizing this book, I came across an extract from *A Cornish Chorus* by Bernard Moore, written around 100 years ago, and republished by Regional Railways in a leaflet promoting 'The Looe Valley Line'. As one whose daily round often includes a journey into London, albeit by the Metropolitan Line and not on what appears to be the South Eastern Railway as described in the poem, I can fully empathise with the sentiments expressed therein and could not resist quoting it in my own work.

'Peckham Rye, Loughborough, Elephant, St. Paul's,'
Every morning the porter bawls.
The train grinds out . . . and I gaze on lots
Of sad back gardens and chimney-pots
Factory stacks and smoky haze
Showering smuts on the close-packed ways . . .

But, trapped and prisoned as I may be,
I lift a latch and my thoughts go free,
And once again I am running down
On a winding track from a Cornish town
And I dream the names of the stations through —
'Moorswater, Causeland, Sandplace, Looe.' . . .

The line twists down through patches sweet
Of soft green pasture and waving wheat
And the stream spreads out to a river wide
Where ships creep up at the turn of tide,
Till a tangle of spars on a blue sky spun
Gives me the sign of the journey done,
And I stand contented on the quay
And hear the surging song of the sea.

So runs the dreamlike journey through,
'Moorswater, Causeland, Sandplace, Looe';
But every morning the porter bawls,
'Peckham Rye, Loughborough, Elephant, St. Paul's.'

No. 4508 leaving Liskeard for Looe on 10th July 1955.   *R. C. Riley*

CHAPTER ONE

AN OUTLINE HISTORY
TO 1900

LIKE other minor railways in Cornwall, the branch line of the GWR and, later, British Railways (Western Region) between Liskeard and Looe has its origins in agriculture. The rural area in the vicinity of Liskeard is well cultivated and generally prosperous, whilst the moors to the north of the town were considered to be some of the most profitable grazing in the entire county. Like much of the rest of Cornwall, however, the acid soil in the cultivated areas required dressing to improve its quality, and it was this necessity that brought about the first communications with the outside world. Elsewhere in the county, 'limy' sea sand was employed as the necessary manure, the transportation of which was the rationale for the construction of the Bude Canal and, later, the Bodmin and Wadebridge Railway, the first locomotive-operated railway in Cornwall.

In the south of the county much use was made of limestone brought by sea from quarries in the Plymouth area and transported by packhorse to a series of lime-kilns in the East Looe river valley between Looe and Liskeard. Since about five tons of burnt lime per acre was spread onto the fields in the season, the kilns would be burning continuously during autumn and early winter and trains of packhorses conveyed the lime to the fields. Some sea sand was also brought into the area, having been dredged at Talland and Lantivet Bays and brought by barge to Sandplace, almost the tidal limit of the East Looe river, for distribution to the agricultural hinterland.

By the late eighteenth century, Liskeard had become a prosperous market town, lively in atmosphere and pleasant in appearance. Chartered in 1240 by the brother of Henry III as a free borough, it soon became a stannary town for the payment of dues and taxes on the tin mined in the Cheesewring area. However, by the late eighteenth century, no tin had passed through the town for a great many years and the mines lay dormant. Communication with neighbouring districts was by packhorse over the most appalling roads or by sea via an ancient quay on the river at St. Germans and the recently-built turnpike road from Torpoint.

Connecting Liskeard with the twin towns of Looe is the East Looe river which flows down a twisting valley to join with its twin, the West Looe river, just to the north of Looe. During high tide, at the confluence of the two rivers, a large expanse of water is formed — a 'loch' surrounded by steep, wooded banks — after which the town is reputedly named. Practically the earliest settlement was opposite this junction of the two rivers, in the area of the present town known as Shutta. At what is now known as East Looe, the earliest habitation seems to have been built on a sandbank and was quite possibly shelter for boats and nets belonging to fishermen who lived upstream at the 'vill of Shutta'. By the middle of the thirteenth century, the settlement of East Looe was becoming well established and

within a short time the street plan recognizable to modern eyes had evolved. Constructed largely of stone under slate roofs, the low houses faced away from the sea, which provided the principal livelihood of its inhabitants. Neighbouring West Looe across the river developed quite separately, being known originally as the 'vill of Portbyham'.

Initially, communication between the twin towns was by ferry or, at low tide, a ford, but by about 1450 the river had been bridged by a stone structure of 15 arches. By the fifteenth century, the town's prosperity depended on fishing, seafaring and shipbuilding although the area of countryside between Looe and Fowey was described as 'fertile, growing corn and grass'.

In the middle of the 16th century, a new deep-water trade emerged which engaged many West Country mariners and the merchants and ship-owners of Looe partook of it fully. In simple terms, the Newfoundland trade was cyclic whereby ships took cargoes of supplies across the Atlantic, loaded the plentiful dried and salted cod caught on the Newfoundland banks, transported it back to Mediterranean Europe, where it found a ready market, and loaded fruit for the freight back to England. It was a prosperous business fully occupying the ports of Looe and Fowey, as well as many others, which lasted until well into the twentieth century before it died away.

In 1588 the residents of West Looe were able to stand on the cliffs, at the area of downs now known as Hannafore and watch the majestic might of the Spanish Armada as it made its way up the channel, with Drake's ships from Plymouth harrying and pursuing the great fleet to its destiny.

In the years following the Civil War, during which the fighting seems to have bypassed Looe, came the Monmouth rebellion which had a rather more profound effect on West Country inhabitants. Fortunately, for many Cornishmen, the local gentry organized resistance to the invading force and most would-be rebels were prevented from joining the Duke's ill-fated army. Prominent amongst these landowners was Sir Jonathan Trelawney, of Trelawne, near West Looe. In later years, he became, in turn, the Bishop of Bristol and of Exeter and was the subject of the famous 'Song of the Western Men'. He lies in the churchyard at the nearby village of Pelynt.

The twin boroughs of East and West Looe continued to expand and prosper throughout the 17th and 18th centuries influenced but slightly by great events elsewhere and preoccupied with their own affairs. By the 1770s, a substantial traffic in limestone from Plymouth quarries at Cattedown and Oreston had built up, as the powdered stone, along with seaweed, sand, waste pilchards and spent salt was in great demand by local farmers in Looe and the surrounding area.

As early as 1777, a canal linking Looe with Liskeard and its agricultural hinterland was proposed but came to nothing, as did a second proposal in 1795. In 1823 a meeting was held in Liskeard to consider 'the improvement of the communication between these two towns; either by a Turnpike Road, a Rail Road, or Canal, from Looe, by Sandplace, to Looe Mills'. Sufficient support was forthcoming for a Bill to be placed before Parliament and the Royal Assent was duly received on 22nd June 1825 authorising construction of the Liskeard and Looe Union Canal.

The route was to run on the west side of the East Looe River as far as Trussell Bridge — near the site of the present St. Keyne station — before crossing the river and running thence on the east side to Moorswater, very slightly to the south of the originally proposed terminus at Looe Mills. Construction commenced within months of the Act and progressed relatively uneventfully although there were some difficulties in obtaining land at the south end of the canal. The landowner was holding out for greater compensation and in the event John Buller, MP for Exeter and owner of a large estate at Morval, near Looe, allowed the canal to be built on his land to the east of the river. The canal was partially in use by 1827 and, as a consequence, the price of coal in Liskeard dropped sharply. Although it is recorded as being fully in use soon after this date, some works were not completed until 1830, notably a reservoir at Moorswater.

Once the canal was open, the Committee of Management set about making improvements to the roads around Moorswater to facilitate distribution of the lime and seasand brought up from Looe. Authority for these works was contained in the Act of Parliament and in 1829 an important road was constructed connecting Moorswater with Liskeard, having gradients of between 1 in 19 and 1 in 29. It remained in the control of the Canal Company until 1881 when Liskeard Borough Council took over responsibility for it. In due course the road became part of the A38 trunk road until the 1970s when the Liskeard Bypass was opened, relegating it to a truncated side road. As well as the roads, additions and improvements to the unloading facilities at Moorswater were made. Wharves and quays were constructed and narrow gauge tramways allowed the incoming limestone to be taken from the waterside to the nearby limekilns.

Traffic on the canal was almost entirely in one direction and consisted principally of limestone, sand and house coal, with little cargo travelling down the canal to Looe. It took eight hours for the carriers' and merchants' own boats to work along the canal, each boat carrying 16 tons of cargo. A 'check' for each vessel was obtained from the company's clerk at Looe, which had to be surrendered on entering the canal at Terras for the appropriate toll to be levied.

In the early 1830s, the area around Caradon Hill, some 4-5 miles to the north of Liskeard, was open moorland providing only grazing for sheep and cattle. Some desultory

exploration for copper ore had taken place with minimal result, and it was generally considered that, other than a little tin, there was no mineral wealth of any consequence to be found in the county east of Truro. The lease permitting exploration changed hands a number of times, eventually passing into the hands of a small party of miners headed by Captain James Clymo, and in 1836 a rich vein of copper ore was struck on the south side of Caradon Hill. South Caradon Mine was established by 1837, to be followed by West Caradon in 1840, working the same lode as South Caradon and proving even more profitable. Both mines were soon producing large quantities of ore, all of which had to be transported by packhorse over the poor roads of the district to Moorswater for conveyance by canal to the port of Looe.

So far as the canal company was concerned, the growth of this traffic was particularly welcome as the mid-1830s brought a slump in agriculture and a decline in the carriage of lime and other manures. In due course, the copper ore was to prove far more lucrative than manure ever had, whilst in 1839 traffic down the canal was given yet further impetus when work commenced to quarry granite near the Cheesewring at Stows Hill, about a mile north of Caradon Hill. By 1840, the traffic emanating from the Caradon copper mines and the Cheesewring quarry far exceeded the capacity of the poor roads in the locality — most of which were impassable in winter — as well as the facilities at the upper terminus of the canal at Moorswater.

By 1842 an agreement had been reached, between the proprietors of the Liskeard and Looe Union Canal and the owners of the South and West Caradon mines, to construct a railway 'between the Liskeard Canal and the Caradon Mines, Cheesewring and Tokenbury'. A sinuous 6½ mile route was proposed, with a ruling gradient of 1 in 60, the traffic being worked by gravity without the aid of locomotives.

Royal Assent for the Liskeard and Caradon Railway Act was sanctioned on 27th June 1843. The line was to be of standard 4ft 8½in gauge and run from the canal basin at Moorswater, via Tremabe, St. Cleer and Crows Nest to the mines at South Caradon. Powers were also contained in the Act for an extension of the main line in due course to Tokenbury Corner, and a branch, via a 1 in 11 inclined plane at Gonamena, to the Cheesewring Quarry. As with the canal, tolls were levied according to the cargo, the Act requiring that milestones be established at every quarter mile along the line and boards erected at each depot listing the tolls.

Construction work on the line commenced early in 1844 at the upper end of the line near the Cheesewring Quarry. The quarry was the source of the stone blocks upon which the rails were to be laid, whilst the rails themselves arrived by sea at Looe and were conveyed free of charge by the canal company to Moorswater. Onward conveyance of the rails from the canal terminus to the construction site on the open moors around Caradon Hill must have been a major achievement given the poor state of the roads.

By November 1844, the line was opened from the Cheesewring for three miles, down as far as Tremabe. Only limited traffic was conveyed at first — the bother of trans-shipping a cargo, after only three miles by rail, for the remaining three miles by road — meant that the majority of output from the mines continued to be conveyed by horse and cart, the railway remaining little used. Eventually, problems in obtaining land at the lower end of the line were overcome and construction was completed. Opening took place in March 1846.

Traffic, when it started, was worked by gravity, the loaded wagons running down individually in the late afternoon and evening, each under the control of a brakesman. In the morning they were hauled back to the mines and quarry workings by horses hired by the company. Since traffic flowed in one direction only at a time, there were no passing loops anywhere on the line.

The new railway was physically isolated from the remainder of Britain's railway system, having been built solely as an adjunct to the canal, but almost as soon as the L & C was opened to traffic, the possibility arose of a connection being made. On 3rd August 1846, the Bill for the construction of the Cornwall Railway received Royal Assent. The railway was authorised to run from a junction with the South Devon Railway at Plymouth, to the packet port of Falmouth. Powers were also contained in the Act to connect with the Liskeard and Caradon Railway and to purchase or lease both it and the Liskeard and Looe Union Canal. In the event, the costs in constructing the main line far exceeded the original estimates and the Cornwall Railway's aspirations had to be considerably curtailed. It was the period of 'Railway Mania' and the difficulties in raising additional capital meant the abandonment of the connection with the L & C and other schemes which were sanctioned in 1852. When the Cornwall Railway eventually opened in May 1859, it was a broad gauge 7ft 0¼in line, which passed above the L & C by means of the 147ft high Moorswater viaduct. Built of timber, to Brunel's distinctive 'fan' viaduct design used throughout the length of the Cornwall Railway, the structure was another example of the economies necessitated by the lack of funds. So far as the L & C was concerned, it had to wait for more than half a century before connection was made with the successor to the Cornwall Railway, the GWR.

Almost from the outset of operations in 1846, the Liskeard and Caradon Railway was profitable. With easier access to the canal at Moorswater, many more mines were established around Caradon and by the early 1850s there were over twenty-five at work. Existing villages grew enormously to accommodate the influx of miners and their families whilst entirely new settlements evolved at Darite, Railway Terrace and the curiously named Minions. Liskeard

was the nearest large town and its population expanded by 50% in only twenty years. As well as the enormous traffic in ore and granite down the canal to Looe, there was a heavy upwards traffic to Moorswater, principally in coal to feed the furnaces of the many engines at work in the mines. Extra wharves were constructed at Moorswater but there were also severe problems at Looe.

The small harbour was quite unable to cope with the influx of traffic; it was, after all, little more than a fishing village which had been in decline for many years following the loss of its pilchard trade during the Napoleonic Wars. The quays were inadequate and the harbour badly silted. In 1848 the East and West Looe Harbour and Bridge Act was obtained, establishing the Looe Harbour Commissioners, and work started almost immediately on a new breakwater at the entrance to the harbour and on new quays.

In due course, the bridge connecting the twin towns, dating from the fifteenth century, was replaced by the present structure erected about 100 yards upstream.

Although, by the mid-1850s, the problems with the harbour facilities at Looe were being dealt with, there were still problems at Moorswater with the interchange between railway wagon and canal boat. Extra land was acquired for stacking ore awaiting shipment, and by 1856 the Committee of Management decided that the canal had reached the limit of its capacity and drastic measures were called for. A first suggestion was to extend the canal from Terras to Looe but on 10th June 1857 the Committee asked two of the canal engineers to prepare an estimate for the construction of a railway from Moorswater to Looe. Running from an end-on connection with the Liskeard and Caradon Railway at Moorswater, the line was to run alongside the canal to Terras and then take a route along the eastern shore of the East Looe river estuary to Looe. At this stage it was intended that the canal should continue to function.

The new line was to be financed by the canal company and costs could be kept low as it owned most of the necessary land. An initial proposal to build a branch to West Looe was not proceeded with as the Canal Committee felt the expenditure to be unjustified.

The Bill passed through Parliament virtually unopposed and the Liskeard and Looe Railway Act received the Royal Assent on 11th May 1858. Construction began almost immediately with rails being purchased from ironworks in South Wales and stone blocks from the Cheesewring Quarry. Silvanus W. Jenkin — one of the two canal company engineers that had prepared the estimates for construction — was appointed Engineer of the new line and had previously been involved in the construction of the broad gauge Cornwall Railway. Probably influenced by this experience, he proposed that the line below Tregarland as far as Looe, should be constructed of bridge rail laid on longitudinal timber sleepers following the practice adopted on the main line. Inevitably, the construction costs exceeded the estimates and additional borrowing powers had to be obtained. Construction work took a little over two years and by December 1860 it was decided that the line was ready for opening. It was proposed that the new line would be worked by locomotive power and as early as May of 1860 negotiations were underway to obtain a steam locomotive. Due to the additional costs in construction, it was decided to hire a locomotive rather than purchase one, whilst the Liskeard and Caradon Railway would supply the trucks.

In the meantime, the continuing increase in traffic over the L & C combined with the forthcoming opening of the L & L, persuaded the directors of the Liskeard and Caradon Railway that they should introduce locomotive power. An Act was obtained on 15th May 1860 which empowered the L & C to obtain capital to improve their line to allow it to accept locomotives, to build the line from Crows Nest to Tokenbury and to realign the Cheesewring branch to ease the Gonamena Incline.

When the Liskeard and Looe Railway opened on 27th December 1860, the company hired the locomotive *Liskeard* which apparently worked well enough for the company to purchase it in 1861. The L & C, however, decided from the outset to purchase their own locomotive and the 0—6—0ST *Caradon* arrived from Gilkes, Wilson & Co of Middlesborough in 1862. In the same year the Liskeard & Caradon Railway Co and the Liskeard and Looe Union Canal Co. formed a joint committee to operate the two railways. It was decided that the L & C would work all traffic over both lines and tolls were fixed from the mines and quarries through to the sea at Looe. A locomotive shed had been built at Moorswater in 1861 to accommodate *Liskeard* and when *Caradon* arrived in 1862 the L & C also purchased *Liskeard*. Both locomotives worked the traffic between Caradon and Looe but horse working also continued on the L & C for some time.

Traffic in copper ore over both railways reached a peak in 1863 and the following year a second locomotive was purchased from Gilkes, Wilson & Co. Again an

An 1870s view of Terras Crossing, near Looe.

Typical length of permanent way with flange rails on stone sleeper blocks. This view was taken near St. Cleer in 1902.   *L & GRP*

Official portraits of the three Liskeard and Caradon Railway locomotives taken at Moorswater at an unknown date.   *National Railway Museum*

The derelict Caradon mines photographed on 23th June 1934.

L & GRP

0−6−0ST, the new engine was named *Cheesewring* and was possibly intended as a replacement for *Liskeard* which was by now life-expired and was later sold.

It had not been the intention for the Liskeard and Looe Railway to supersede the canal, but, not surprisingly, this is what happened. Almost immediately it started to fall into disuse and only the lower section from Terras Pill to Sandplace carried any traffic. An agreement with the local landowner, John Buller of Morval, required that the canal provide toll-free access for his or his tenants' boats to the quays at Sandplace, and the canal committee were obliged to continue to allow this until the early years of the twentieth century. Indeed, between 1862 and 1867 money was spent on repairs to the section of canal below Sandplace.

Throughout the 1860s, the amount of traffic was often beyond the capacity of two locomotives and in 1869 a third was purchased, another 0−6−0ST, this time named *Kilmar*. However, by the time it arrived, traffic over the line was beginning to decline. A number of mines around Caradon Hill had closed, although a branch was laid to Phoenix Mine, replacing a narrow gauge tramway, whilst those remaining were asking for a reduction in tolls. Granite traffic from the Cheesewring and Kilmar quarries continued but other sources of income were sought. There was a scheme to extend the L & C line northward to link with a proposed LSWR line into Cornwall, intended to connect with the Bodmin & Wadebridge Railway which

When this photograph was taken on 11th July 1986 a few rails remained in situ at the entrance to the disused Cheesewring Quarry. The Cheesewring itself is prominent on the skyline.
Author

The disused formation of the 1877 line from Crows Nest to Tokenbury Corner and Minions, photographed in 1934. *L & GRP*

the LSWR had owned since 1846. It was also resolved to extend the line from Tokenbury Corner around Caradon Hill to connect with the Cheesewring branch, thus doing away with the Gonamena Incline which was proving an obstacle to the efficient working of the line. In the event, the proposal to extend northwards came to nothing whilst the extension of the line around Caradon Hill commenced in 1872, but work ceased soon after due to lack of funds. Construction recommenced in 1876 and the line was opened by August 1877, the Gonamena Incline being closed simultaneously.

By the mid 1870s it became obvious that the boom in mining around Caradon Hill had passed and the Liskeard and Caradon Railway was seeking to increase its hold on the Liskeard and Looe line, particularly as it was proposed to start a passenger service to Looe. The L & C had worked the L & L for ten years or more and it was considered that the acquisition of the L & L would offset the decline in revenue from mineral traffic. Negotiations commenced in 1877 and on 29th January 1878 the Liskeard and Looe line was leased to the Liskeard & Caradon Railway. Unusually, the line was administered by a Management Committee and not a Board of Directors whilst the title of the railway remained the Liskeard & Looe Union Canal. The L & C took control on 27th February 1878, the

revenue to be apportioned according to the mileage worked over each company's lines and 50% of the gross earnings of traffic working over the L & LUC line being paid to that company.

Although proposals had been made as early as 1865, it was not until 1879 that action was taken to introduce a passenger service between Moorswater and Looe. Previously passengers had been carried over both railways by the mineral trains on an unofficial basis. Colonel Rich made an inspection of the Looe line in April 1879 to advise the Management Committee of the work necessary to upgrade the line to make it suitable for working passenger trains. As might be expected, much work was required including renewal of the permanent way, provision of signals, mileposts, booking offices, waiting rooms, clocks, nameboards and urinals. Some of the overbridges gave concern, being considered a little weak and too narrow to accept 'normal coaching stock'.

By August, however, the required work had been done and on 7th September 1879 Colonel Rich again inspected the line. Stations were provided at Moorswater, Causeland and Looe, whilst a goods siding was also provided at Sandplace where a passenger station was opened later in 1881. The Colonel sanctioned the opening of the line for passenger traffic providing that the L & CR worked trains to a maximum speed of 20 mph and undertook to work the line on a one-engine-in-steam basis. The required undertaking was given and the passenger service commenced on 11th September. Whilst he was in the area, the Colonel was asked to give an opinion on the suitability of the L & C line for establishing a similar service, and although he gave a generally favourable response, the proposal was not proceeded with due to the expense in upgrading the line.

Around Caradon Hill, the mines had continued to decline, suffering from a depression in world copper prices, and many of the miners left the area to find a new life in the Americas. During the winter of 1881/2 work at the quarries at Cheesewring and Kilmar ceased as cheaper supplies of granite were discovered in Scotland, Norway and Sweden. Little traffic was being conveyed over the L & C and the directors again searched for fresh sources of traffic. Plans were again prepared to extend the line northwards toward Trewint whilst a further attempt was to be made to join up with the Cornwall main line at Liskeard. Passing unopposed through Parliament, the Liskeard and Caradon Railway Act 1882 received the Royal Assent on 12th July 1882 formalising lines already built and authorising the raising of capital. Construction work did not commence immediately on the 'northern extension' as it became known, although the route was staked out, and

when additional powers were sought in 1884 to extend the Trewint line to Launceston, both the GWR and the LSWR opposed it. Eventually, Parliament authorised the Trewint to Launceston line but little, if any, construction work was done, principally due to difficulties in raising the necessary capital.

At around the same time, the well-known practice of conveying passengers by goods train free and charging them for the carriage of belongings started. Possibly the practice commenced at the suggestion of Colonel Rich who had made a further examination of the L & C line with a view to operating passenger trains. Certainly disclaimer notices were erected at Looe, Sandplace, Moorswater, Polwrath, Tokenbury* and Rillaton and the practice appears to have continued until about 1896 when the L & C permanent way became unsafe, only mineral trains being conveyed thereafter.

In 1885 the formerly wealthy South Caradon mine ceased operations and traffic on the L & C was the lowest it had been for many years although some work had commenced on the extension to Trewint. However, whilst the L & C directors continued their attempts to raise the capital to fund their aspirations northwards, the banks were

*The notice from Tokenbury is preserved in the Great Western Railway Museum at Swindon.

Moorswater station, photographed c.1890 and probably little different from when it opened in 1879.   *L & GRP*

demanding payment of outstanding debts. The company could do little to counter this threat and on 13th October 1886 the Liskeard and Caradon Railway entered into receivership.

Economies were introduced immediately. What little work had commenced on the Trewint extension ceased forthwith, never to be resumed, wages and salaries were cut and redundancies made. By 1887 only two trains per day worked on the Looe line — with extras on market days — and only two trains per day from Moorswater to Caradon — and then only if six or more wagons were to be conveyed.

The decline in mining operations around Caradon Hill was the principal reason for the reduction in the fortunes of the L & C. Although there was a brief resurgence in world prices of copper in 1889, which gave hopes to the

area, it was shortlived and at the start of the 1890s the mines were moribund. Only the Phoenix United mine was at work extracting tin which, as it was processed at the mine, provided little traffic for the railway — along with granite from the Cheesewring Quarry — and the L & C managed to eke out an existence until the end of the century. It was the passenger traffic between Moorswater and Looe which provided the only real source of revenue and, with maintenance of the permanent way reduced to the minimum, the track on both railways deteriorated badly. Phoenix United ceased work in 1898, leaving the Cheesewring Quarry as the only customer for the L & C. The future for either of the railways did not, on the surface, appear to be bright but events were already unfolding which were to transform the fortunes of the Looe line.

An undated but early view of the terminus at Looe with a semaphore starting signal at the end of the platform.

Collection Robert Tivendale

CHAPTER TWO

THE LISKEARD AND LOOE EXTENSION RAILWAY

AS has already been related, when the Cornwall Railway line between Plymouth and Truro was opened on 2nd May 1859, it consisted of a single track of broad gauge metals with crossing places at all stations. Liskeard was provided with a station from the outset and, as well as the loop which permitted the crossing of up and down trains, there was a goods yard and a small locomotive shed. The Cornwall Railway's continuous problems with finances eventually brought about the involvement of the GWR and the other broad gauge companies, the Bristol and Exeter Railway and the South Devon Railway, to the extent that the Cornwall Railway was managed by a Joint Committee. By 1876 the GWR had assumed control of the three West of England broad gauge companies through amalgamation, and Executive Officers of the GWR were appointed to equivalent positions on the Cornwall Railway.

There were two of Brunel's timber 'fan' viaducts in the vicinity of Liskeard station. Immediately to the east of the station is the Liskeard viaduct whilst a short distance to the west, and spanning the upper limits of the East Looe river and the Liskeard and Looe Union Canal, stands the well-known Moorswater viaduct. As early as 1871 the expenditure of maintaining the viaducts was giving cause for concern given the parlous financial situation of the Cornwall Railway. There were 34 on the main line between Plymouth and Truro and work started on converting them, some of the smaller ones being replaced by embankments whilst others were replaced by masonry structures or rebuilt with wrought iron decks resting on the original modified piers. In 1881 Moorswater viaduct was replaced by a new stone structure built to the standard width for a double narrow gauge line. Initially, however, it carried a single broad gauge line and was built alongside the original using material taken from the railway company's own quarry near Menheniot station.

Throughout the 1880s the Cornwall Railway made overtures to the GWR to take the company over and eventually terms were agreed which the Cornwall Railway Board could recommend to its shareholders. On 21st June 1889 the

Moorswater viaduct with the works of the Cheesewring Granite Company below. The stone piers which supported the previous Brunel timber viaduct are visible behind.

Author's collection

A pre-1892 broad gauge view of the east end of Liskeard station. The line in the foreground gave access to Isaac's siding.
Liskeard Old Cornwall Society

The west end of Moorswater viaduct with a GWR broad gauge train heading for Doublebois. Moorswater signal box of the Liskeard and Caradon Railway may be seen in the valley below.
Liskeard Old Cornwall Society

affairs of the Cornwall Railway were wound up at a special general meeting and, as from 1st July 1889, the Cornwall Railway became an integral part of the GWR empire.

It had been obvious for a number of years that the days of the broad gauge were numbered — the costs of conversion thus involved were reason enough for the Cornwall Railway to sell out to the GWR, and with this event ever more likely to occur, there emerged further proposals to connect the Liskeard and Looe Railway with its important neighbour. The first of the new proposals was made in 1888 by Joseph Thomas, a civil engineer of considerable repute, who wished to improve the prospects of the area in which he had spent his childhood. Initially it was proposed to run the connecting line from Lodge — south of the site later occupied by Coombe Junction — up and across the Liskeard valley to enter the main line station from the south-east. As this scheme involved a large viaduct, it was considered too costly and was not proceeded with, neither was a second proposal in 1890 which included a rack railway on the Rigenbach principle from Moorswater!

A third proposal was made by Thomas in 1892 which envisaged a line diverging from the Liskeard and Looe line at Trussell bridge (close to the site presently occupied by St. Keyne station), climbing at 1 in 40 through Lamellion and passing beneath the GWR Moorswater viaduct at the east end to halt at a reversing spur near the workhouse. The route continued in the opposite direction at a gradient of 1 in 45 to connect with the goods yard at the west end of the GWR Liskeard station. This plan seems to have been favourably received by the Committee of Management of the canal company but was not proceeded with.

Also in 1892 the remaining obstacle in connecting the two railways, so far as the GWR was concerned, was removed when the broad gauge was abolished on the main line between Exeter and Truro. Details of the gauge conversion epic have been recorded elsewhere and suffice it to say here that this major civil engineering feat was accomplished over the weekend of 20th and 21st May 1892. The last up broad gauge train was a special conveying empty stock to Swindon for scrapping and/or conversion to 'narrow' gauge, and once it had passed each station, work commenced on converting the gauge of the main line. Workmen from all over the GWR system were brought to the West of England for the gauge conversion and in the Liskeard area, men from the Paddington Division assisted the local permanent way gangs in their task. Such was the progress of the work that standard gauge locomotives were testing the line on Sunday, 22nd May, and the normal train service resumed on Monday, 23rd May, using standard gauge rolling stock.

In 1893 Joseph Thomas, a native of Roche, settled in Looe, and began to develop it as a resort. After assisting his father on the reconstruction of Looe bridge, his career had commenced with a London contractor and he worked on the Bovisand Fort at Plymouth and later for the Midland Railway at St. Pancras station. He then went abroad to work on the Eastern Hungarian State Railway and on his return to England was appointed engineer of the abortive Easton and Church Hope Railway on the Isle of Portland in Dorset. His next appointment was to the St. Helier Harbour Works on Jersey where Thomas was responsible for La Corbiere lighthouse. By 1893 Thomas had semi-retired but was appointed engineer responsible for the St. Ives and Mevagissey Harbour Works, and his return to Cornwall enabled him to take a more active part in the development of Looe. The opportunity arose to purchase land at Hannafore suitable for the erection of houses and hotels and this Thomas did as well as constructing a new approach road on the west side of the harbour entrance. Thomas also assisted the Looe Harbour Commissioners in constructing the 'Banjo' pier to protect the entrance to the harbour from the sea and built a new and powerful port light.

Thomas's arrival in the district and his enthusiasm in developing Looe seems to have reinvigorated the Management Committee of the canal company who set about examining their relationship with the Liskeard and Caradon Company. It was their intention to regain their own line from the L & C and to promote the construction of a connecting line to the GWR. In 1895 Thomas made a final proposal for the new line, which was approved and a Bill was laid before Parliament. The Liskeard and Looe Extension Railway Act received the Royal Assent on 6th July 1895 and authorised the construction of a line from Coombe Gate to the GWR Liskeard station and that, on completion of the new railway, the Liskeard and Looe Union Canal would regain control of their railway, would take over the locomotives, rolling stock and other assets of the Liskeard and Caradon Railway which remained in receivership, and would work the L & C line. In addition, the name of the LLUC was to be changed to the Liskeard and Looe Railway.

Joseph Thomas was appointed engineer of the new line but little work was done for two years due to difficulties in raising finances. Eventually a Captain J. E. Spicer of Chippenham was persuaded to take shares in the Liskeard and Looe Railway Company, in effect becoming the owner, although the Management Committee remained in control, and work could commence on construction of the Extension Railway.

The ceremonial first turf was turned by Sylvanus Jenkin, senior engineer of the Liskeard and Looe Railway, on 28th June 1898. According to the *Cornish Times*, 'forthwith some fifty men were put to work by the contractor and operations were pushed forward with vigour during that fine summer, but difficulties, chiefly with the acquisition of the necessary land delayed the completion of the work'. Contractor to the work was the local firm of T. Lang and Son and such was the progress made that the earthworks were complete by the end of 1900 and track-laying was in hand. One of the chief engineering features of the new line was the manner in which it was planned so that the embankments and cuttings alternated, the material taken from one cutting being employed in constructing an

Looe Harbour c.1900.

embankment in the next section. Altogether the amount of material removed to form the larger cuttings reached about 160,000 cubic yards, whilst the total bank filling amounted to as much as 192,000 cubic yards. Before work on the line could be completed, it became obvious that the financial position would not permit the line to be finished nor the purchase of new rolling stock. Once again Captain Spicer was prevailed upon, although he had little choice if he was to protect his initial investment. Rails were duly purchased from the Blaenavon Iron Company and a new locomotive and carriages ordered.

Whilst this flurry of activity was going on, an important staff appointment was made when Horace Holbrook was recruited to take the position of Traffic Manager of the revitalised Liskeard and Looe Railway. He came from the Traffic Department of the Great Eastern Railway and a number of other staff came with him from that company, including A. Burridge and H. Hawkes who became the station masters at Liskeard and Looe respectively. Holbrook's appointment took effect on 2nd January 1901 and initially his salary was fixed at £200 per annum.

By February 1901 the construction work was complete and the L&LR notified the Board of Trade that the line was ready for inspection prior to the commencement of a passenger service. By 25th February the GWR had made the physical connection between the two companies and the points and catchpoints controlling entry and exit to the new line were connected to the GWR signal box. The inspection for the Board of Trade was carried out by Col. H. A. Yorke on 1st March and his report read thus:

RAILWAY DEPARTMENT
Board of Trade
8 Richmond Terrace
Whitehall, London, SW

March 18, 1901

Sir,

I have the honour to report for the information of the Board of Trade, that in compliance with the instructions contained in your Minute of the 26th July I inspected on the 1st March the Liskeard and Looe Railway extension.

This line commences by a junction with the existing Looe Railway at Coombe level crossing, and terminates at the new station at Liskeard, which has been constructed close to the station belonging to the GW Ry. at the former place. Its length is 1 mile 7 furlongs 3 chains; the gauge is 4ft 8½in and it is single throughout, except at the junction at Coombe and at Liskeard stations, at both of which places loop lines have been laid in to enable engines to run round their trains.

No land has been purchased for an additional line of rails. The width at formation level is 17ft on embankment and 16ft in cutting.

The sharpest curve has a radius of 8 chains, and the steepest gradient which extends for 1¼ miles, an inclination of 1 in 40.

The cuttings and embankments are heavy. The deepest cutting has a depth of 52ft and the highest embankment a height of 62ft.

The permanent way is laid with bull-headed steel rails weighing 77½lbs per yard, cast iron chains weighing 36lbs each, and creosoted sleepers 9ft x 10in x 5in. The ballast consists of broken stone, and there is plenty of it.

The track is in excellent order and suitable for passenger traffic.

There are 4 bridges over the line, all built with brick arches and stone abutments, and there are two bridges under the line, one being an arched, and the other a girder bridge. There is also a culvert 5ft wide, with a flat top consisting of rolled steel joists embedded in a slab of concrete 14 inches thick.

As regards the culvert the joists are not sufficient in themselves to carry the load, and it is impossible to apportion the

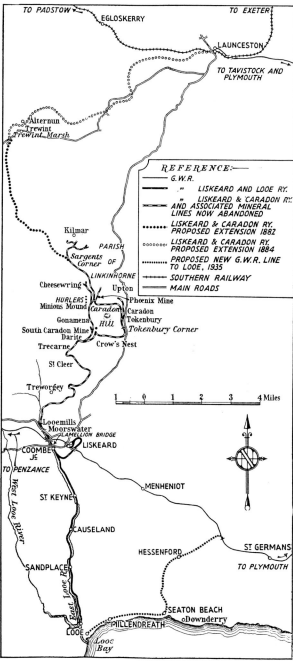

Sketch map of the Liskeard & Caradon and Liskeard & Looe Railways

Cty. Railway Magazine

An undated view near Sandplace of *Cheesewring* with much of the Liskeard and Caradon Railway rolling stock.   *Author's collection*

weights to be carried or the work to be done between the joists and the concrete. Although this culvert showed no deflection under test and probably possesses sufficient practical strength, there is no means of arriving at its theoretical strength. For these reasons the engineer of the company has agreed at my recommendation to build a centre pier, thus halving the span, and enabling the steel joists if necessary to carry the entire load.

The under bridge has steel girders carrying jack arches, and it possesses sufficient theoretical strength, and gave no appreciable deflection when tested with the company's present engine.

There are two new stations, viz Coombe and Liskeard. The first of these is not, strictly speaking, situated on the new (Liskeard & Looe Extension) railway, being on the old Looe Railway, a short distance north of the junction of the new and old lines. It forms however a part of the new scheme for the working of the railway and may be conveniently reported upon here. It is to take the place of the existing station at Moorswater and consists of a single platform sufficiently long to accommodate four of the coaches of the Liskeard & Looe railway.

It possesses neither booking office nor conveniences. This station does not conform to the standard requirements of the Board of Trade which are hardly applicable to the peculiar conditions existing here. Few if any passengers will make use of this station which only exists because, in consequence of the steep gradient to Liskeard, it is necessary to have a reversing place for trains. As therefore trains are compelled to stop at this place, while their engines change from one end to the other, it is convenient to the persons employed in the adjacent manufactory to be permitted to enter or leave the trains. Any tickets required to be issued, will be obtained from the guard, and arrangements will be made for lighting the station after dark. Under the special circumstances, I am of opinion that this

Guard Joseph Uren joined the Liskeard and Caradon Railway in 1860 at the age of 18 and retired in 1902.   *L & GRP*

Kilmar with a passenger train at Looe.
Author's collection

station may be approved for present use on the condition that if at any future time the company are called upon by the Board of Trade to increase the accommodation, they shall do so.

Liskeard station consists of a single platform 60 yards long, on which there are booking hall, waiting rooms, ladies room, and conveniences for both sexes.

The line is to be worked on the electric tablet system, and signal boxes have been erected at Liskeard & Coombe. An undertaking as to the mode of working the line should be furnished by the Company to the Board of Trade in accordance with Board of Trade Requirement C. If, as I understand, it is the intention of the Company to work the existing line as between Looe & Coombe by means of the electric tablet, an undertaking to that effect should also be forwarded, and the existing undertaking whereby the old line is to be worked by one engine in steam &c should be cancelled.

The signalling arrangements at Liskeard are operated from the signal box, which contains 18 levers (of which 13 are in use and 5 are spare) and a gate wheel.

The only requirement at this place is that a bar should be attached to No. 15 points, so as to work in conjunction with them, and prevent any risk of the points being moved while a train is passing through them.

At Coombe the signal box contains 26 levers (of which 20 are in use and 6 spare) and a gate wheel.

The requirements I noted at Coombe are (1) No. 1 signal lever not to be released by Nos. 13 and 14; (2) in consequence of the gradient a runaway siding to be laid in on the new line with points facing to trains from Liskeard, these points to be normally for the siding and to be interlocked with the signals, & the siding to be made as long as possible and to be either level or on a gradient ascending from the junction with the main line.

The signalling arrangements at both Liskeard and Coombe, but more particularly at the latter, are, I consider, unnecessarily elaborate. For instance at both places the roads crossed by the railway are either private or accommodation roads, and there was no necessity for the gates to be opened and closed by means of apparatus in the signal boxes, the cost of the mechanism required for the purpose being out of all proportion to the advantage gained in such places at these. Safety could have been

obtained by a simple bolt on the gates, the bolt being operated by lever interlocked with the signals.

At Coombe the arrangements at the level crossing comprise the existing occupation gates of ordinary design opening outwards from the line as required by the Act of 1845, in addition to which there are, as just stated, two gates, each with two wings operated from the signal box.

The signals at Coombe are also more numerous than necessary, and the proposed system of working each line being signalled for both directions, more elaborate than desirable. Having regard to the amount of traffic likely to pass over the railway, simpler arrangements and fewer signals would have been accepted by an inspecting officer of the B of Trade.

I draw attention to this matter because it is often stated that the Board of Trade compel railway companies to erect costly and unnecessary signalling installations. Here, at any rate, the Company have voluntarily adopted a more elaborate system than would have been imposed on them by the Board of Trade.

Summing up, the following are the requirements specified in this report:

(1) A bar to be fitted to No. 15 points at Liskeard;
(2) A centre pier to be built under the girders of Coombe culvert;
(3) Undertakings to be furnished as to the mode of working;
(4) At Coombe signal box No. 1 lever not to be released by Nos. 13 & 14;
(5) A runaway catch siding to be laid in on the Liskeard line.

Subject to these requirements, to which the Company have assented, being completed within the following periods viz, as to 3 one week; as to 1, 2, 4, 5 one month, I can recommend the Bd. of Trade to sanction the use of the line between Liskeard & Coombe for passenger traffic, but owing to the gradient the speed of trains travelling downhill, i.e. from Liskeard towards Coombe, should not exceed 10 miles an hour.

I have &C, &c
(signed) H. A. Yorke

In the meantime goods trains began using the new line on 25th February, and on 9th April 1901 the Liskeard & Looe Company informed the BoT that they had given the

Liskeard and Caradon Company the required one month's notice that they (the L&LR) were to take over running their railway on 8th May when they also intended opening the Liskeard and Looe Extension Railway. The old Liskeard and Caradon Railway rolling stock was used for the first week of passenger operation over the new line, the recently arrived locomotive *Looe* and the new 'American style' coaches being saved for the official opening on 15th May.

The usual celebrations accompanied the formal opening and the official train was met on arrival at Looe by a gathering of civil dignitaries. A procession through the decorated streets to a reception at the Guildhall was accompanied by the Liskeard Borough Band and 400 children. On the quay a marquee was erected in which many of the public were entertained to luncheon and speeches. During the celebrations, tributes were paid to Joseph Thomas and a silver bowl was presented in recognition of his services, not only in promoting the new railway but also to the Harbour Commissioners and for other works around Looe. Many people travelled between the two towns and in addition a large party came by train from Plymouth. Many remained in Looe until the evening and left by the 8.35 p.m. train, but after leaving Coombe Junction, the new engine ran out of steam on the steep gradient. Assistance arrived promptly but when the train reached Liskeard, the Plymouth-bound passengers found they had missed the last GWR train in that direction. Horace Holbrook immediately arranged with the GWR station master for the 10.26 p.m. arrival from Plymouth to return there as a special. The Liskeard and Looe Railway met the entire cost of the special train but must have accrued much goodwill by this action.

The *Cornish Times* reported extensively on these events in its edition of 18th May 1901. The report also carried a detailed description of the new line, which read thus:

'The course followed by the new extension line is necessarily a circuitous one. The original line is left at Coombe, a point about a quarter of a mile below Moorswater and well within view of the high viaduct which then carries the Great Western line over the valley. The sight of this great bridge, nearly 200ft above the Looe line demonstrates clearly the magnitude of the task the engineer set himself to climb to the level of the main line within a reasonable distance. At Coombe where there is a level crossing leading from the highway to Coombe House, the old canal was diverted and the original channel filled in for some distance in order to carry the new line which begins to mount at once. Over Coombe Lane it is carried by a stone bridge and then traverses Mr. Milton's plantation, curving steadily to the left, and passing under the road at Lodge Hill by means of another stone bridge, the construction of which was carried out without interference with the ordinary highway traffic. On the other side of the road a deep cutting through solid rock was entered upon, and it was two years and four months before this difficult portion of the work was completed, the cutting being one of the deepest in Cornwall. It was here also that the only fatality occurred, a poor young fellow sustaining injuries through a fall of rock. All this way the line has been rising at a gradient of 1 in 40, and at Lodge Hill takes its first big sweep to the left on a curve of

Kilmar at Looe. The large cab is thought to have been provided in 1902 whilst the brake van was acquired from the GWR in 1903.
Author's collection

Looe off the road at Coombe Junction in 1902.
Collection Robert Tivendale

10½ chains radius. Entering the Liskeard valley, the line is carried over an embankment some 60ft in height, and passes underneath the Liskeard Viaduct of the GWR between the second and third piers from the eastern end and at a depth of 80ft to 90ft below Liskeard station, the point to be reached. The method adopted for mounting the remaining distance is one of the engineering triumphs of the little line. The contour of the country was carefully studied by the engineer, who has utilised the slopes of the Bolitho Valley to carry the line. A fairly lengthy cutting through the Bolitho Fields takes the railway along the eastern side of the valley, and from that point it makes a second big sweep to the left on an 8-chain curve, mounting gradually, with an alternate cutting and filling, until by means of a small embankment it is carried on to the western side of the valley, running for a short distance parallel with Gut Lane, and then heading straight for its destination. The little valley running down from the town of Liskeard is crossed by means of an embankment with a culvert at its foot to take the Pipe Well stream, and then the rails pass below Heathlands Lane, where an overhead bridge carries the road over the line. Up to this point the line has been rising at a gradient of 1 in 60, and the pulling strain on the engine is thus equalised throughout its course. Passing the bridge, the line continues to rise at 1 in 55 to a level crossing between meadows, and by a 1 in 200 to the signal box outside the Liskeard station, where, at an altitude of 335ft above sea level, it forms a junction with the Great Western. The total length of the new line is nearly two miles, to traverse a distance of scarcely three-quarters of a mile as the crow flies, but Coombe and Moorswater are only 130ft above sea level, so that a big detour was necessarily called for in order to make the ascent of 205ft.'

Both passenger and goods/mineral receipts soon fulfilled the expected promise and the connecting line was considered to be a success. In 1900, 21,000 passengers were carried over the line and this figure had risen to 70,798 by 1908. On the old line, however, between Coombe Junction and Looe, the condition of the permanent way was giving much cause for concern. Even before the formal opening of the new line, Thomas had reported to the Management Committee that there were serious defects with the old line, the track being up to 1½ inches wide of gauge in places. Much of the line south of Coombe Junction consisted of old flange rails laid on granite blocks and Thomas stated that 'about 100 rails are entirely worn out and want replacing and a good part requires ballasting'. South of the 3 mile stone most of the line was of bridge rail laid on longitudinal sleepers, of which the rails were worn out, the timbers 'thoroughly rotten' and required 'immediate renewal'. Blame for the poor state of the track was laid on the receiver of the L & C who had been responsible for working the Liskeard and Looe line until the Extension railway was opened and Thomas concluded his report:

'It is with much regret that the piece of line from 1½ miles to 2½ miles should have been laid down three years ago with rail sleepers. The rails were brought onto the line before that date for the purpose of relaying this length but as soon as it was known that the L & L Co. was going to make their connecting line with that of the GWR the lengths I now refer to for renewal was stopped and the trains have been allowed to carry passengers over the length of line which is really not safe and the engineer for the line actually giving a certificate that the line was in working order.'

Once the L & L Co. had assumed control of their own line, as an immediate measure, Thomas had the platelayers patch up defects on Sunday 12th May ready for the official opening of the Extension railway but in the longer term he estimated that it would cost around £3,500 to repair the line as well as replacing much of the fencing.

It was not only the condition of the permanent way that was causing concern, for there was also a motive power crisis. The newly acquired locomotive, the 0–6–0ST *Looe*, was proving most unsatisfactory. Its short coupled wheelbase made the locomotive too heavy for the lightly-laid and badly-maintained track between Coombe Junction and Looe and it also had a habit of running short of steam. Its failure on the official opening day has already been mentioned and only a week later it is recorded as derailing itself at Coombe Junction. It was, after all, a shunting locomotive built to a Robert Stephenson standard design and was not really suited to passenger train working. In addition, the old Liskeard and Caradon locomotives, now in

The line south of Sandplace consisted of steel flange rails on creosoted sleepers and was laid c.1899 replacing the original permanent way. This is the view towards Looe early in the 1900s.

E. Pouteau

GWR 4—4—0ST No. 13 at Looe whilst on hire to the L & LR, with the Hurst Nelson built coaches provided for the opening of the L & LER.

the possession of the Liskeard and Looe Railway, were as run down as the permanent way. Both *Cheesewring* and *Kilmer* required repairs and only *Caradon* was in a suitable condition for assisting with the L & L passenger service, to which duties were added such mineral traffic as was forthcoming over the old L & C line. Although unsuitable, *Looe* was working the service in the short term with *Caradon* or *Cheesewring* working 'to the hills' when necessary, but clearly something had quickly to be done. Holbrook went to Paddington and managed to persuade the GWR to loan a locomotive to work the Liskeard–

Looe passenger service. 4–4–0ST No. 13 arrived late in 1901 or early 1902, Holbrook having assured the GWR that the track was in a suitable condition to accept the new arrival. The GWR engine was not permitted to run north of Moorswater, however, over the L & C line, and the L & C locomotives continued to work the Caradon line until it closed.

Although the arrival on loan of No. 13 eased the locomotive situation, there remained the problem of *Looe*, a newly acquired asset that could not be allowed to remain underused. In due course it was sold to the London and

Platform elevation of Looe station building in the early 1900s.
Collection Robert Tivendale

No. 13 standing alongside the carriage shed at Looe during one of its periods of hire.
Author's collection

India Docks Co., which concern already had a number of similar machines successfully in use, and quotes were obtained for a replacement locomotive. The estimate of Andrew Barclay & Co. of Kilmarnock was accepted and Captain Spicer was prevailed upon again to provide the difference between the proceeds from the sale of *Looe* and the cost of its replacement. When the new locomotive arrived in November 1902, it was named *Lady Margaret* in honour of Captain Spicer's wife, and Holbrook was able to report that 'the locomotive is very satisfactory' and that 'we now have a reliable locomotive which can go anywhere and do anything we may require.'

In contrast to the improvements on the Liskeard and Looe line, the little-used Caradon line was suffering from a lack of maintenance and was deteriorating quickly. In 1901 only one train per week was running over the line but the permanent way was not considered safe for even this small amount of traffic. As much as five miles of the main line consisted of badly-worn iron rails resting in small chairs, these in turn being spiked down to stone blocks. The rails were joined by a joint chair and oak keys and were not tied to gauge in any way. Several of the branches to the

quarries and mines also required urgent attention, but the lack of traffic meant they were unlikely to receive it. The L & C line continued in the hands of the receiver and any traffic was worked by the Liskeard and Looe Co. under a working arrangement.

In 1902 a little extra traffic was gained for the Caradon line when the St. Neots China Clay Co. commenced the construction of clay drying sheds at Moorswater. Initially, wagon loads of stone from Cheesewring Quarry and sand from East Caradon were brought down for the building work and in due course a siding was laid to the site of the works by the L & L Co. The clay pit was nine miles away on Bodmin Moor and the clay was piped in the form of slurry to the dries at Moorswater. In due course, additional sidings were provided on Looe Quay, at the expense of the clay company, and the first consignment of clay was sent by rail from Moorswater to Looe for shipment by sea in November 1904.

As for the canal, it was by this date practically moribund, although the railway company remained responsible for the maintenance where it was still navigable. By all accounts, this was very little because when in 1901 Mrs. Tremayne,

This view was taken c.1900 in the sidings at the east end of Liskeard station.   *John L. Rapson, Liskeard Old Cornwall Society*

Lady Margaret with ex-Mersey Railway coaches in the L & LR station at Liskeard, probably around 1905.　　*Collection Robert Tivendale*

the successor to Buller at Morval, who had the right of free carriage of sand along the canal from Looe to Sandplace, wished to exercise her right, she was persuaded to accept carriage by rail to the siding at Sandplace. Apparently the canal was only navigable to Sandplace at extraordinary tides because the poor condition of the gates of the sea-lock at Terras Pill allowed the water to flow in and out with the tide and it could not maintain a satisfactory water level in the canal.

As the new century progressed, work continued on upgrading the permanent way of the Looe line and improvements were made in other respects also. By January 1905 it was reported that some three miles of track remained laid with stone blocks, but a portion of the line had been relaid near Sandplace. The old rails were chiefly of iron and were very worn to the extent that laminations would break away when a train passed. New rails were being laid as fast as they could be provided and at the sharpest curves the gauge was maintained by newly installed wrought-iron tie rods.

A new station was opened at St. Keyne in 1902 in response to a petition from local residents, whilst in 1905 the company published an illustrated poster in full colour extolling the virtues of a holiday in Looe and travel by the Liskeard and Looe Railway. With new and reliable locomotives and rolling stock, permanent way that was

being steadily upgraded, and an enthusiastic and energetic management, the early to mid-1900s might be considered to be the heyday of the independent company. As an illustration of the enterprise shown by Holbrook, the traffic manager, in 1905 he proposed the purchase of a 'road motor' to operate excursions in the area. He reported fully on the road operations of his former employers, the GER, on the Southwold–Kessingland service. In the event, nothing came of this scheme and it was left to others to introduce motor bus services into the district.

By April 1906 over 303,000 passengers had been conveyed over the L & L line since the opening of the Extension railway in May 1901, with an earning of £10,242 16s 8d. On 15th June 1906, however, this feeling of wellbeing was dented when the railway suffered its most serious accident when a train of carriages ran away from the Liskeard terminus. The *Cornish Times* rushed out a special edition and, under the characteristically lurid headlines of the period, gave the following account:

'On Thursday the Company provided a special train, consisting of eleven coaches, to convey the children, teachers and friends of the Looe Wesleyan Sunday School to Liskeard, en route for Doublebois, where, by the kind permission of Mrs. Hermon, the annual outing took place in the beautiful grounds there. The train returned to Looe in the evening, the carriages remaining there the night. Yesterday afternoon five of the carriages which

LISKEARD AND LOOE RAILWAY.

OPENING OF A NEW STATION
AT
ST. KEYNE.

ON MONDAY, SEPTEMBER 1st, 1902, a New Passenger Station (situated between Causeland and Coombe Junction Stations), to be called "ST. KEYNE," will be OPEN FOR TRAFFIC, and all Up and Down Passenger Trains will Stop there for the purpose of picking up and setting down Passengers

On Week Days during the month of September, 1902,

TRAINS WILL DEPART FROM ST. KEYNE AS FOLLOWS:—

FOR LOOE.	FOR LISKEARD.
9 20 A.M. *	9 8 A.M.
10 35 A.M.	12 18 P.M.
1 30 P.M.	2 23 P.M. †
3 15 P.M. †	4 8 P.M.
5 15 P.M.	6 23 P.M.
7 45 P.M.	8 43 P.M. †
9 51 P.M. †	

* TUESDAYS AND SATURDAYS ONLY.   † WEDNESDAYS AND SATURDAYS ONLY.

THE FOLLOWING LOCAL FARES WILL BE IN OPERATION, VIZ:—

BETWEEN ST. KEYNE AND	SINGLE.			RETURN.		
	1st.	2nd.	3rd.	1st.	2nd.	3rd.
	s. d.	s. d.	s. d.	s. d.	s. d.	s. d.
CAUSELAND	- 3	- 2½	- 1½	- 5	- 3	———
COOMBE	- 6	- 4	- 2	- 9	- 6	———
LISKEARD	- 10	- 6	- 3½	1 2	- 10	- 7
LOOE.................................	1 0	- 7	- 5	1 7	1 0	- 10
SANDPLACE	- 6	- 4	- 3	- 10	- 6	———

NOTE.—3RD RETURN TICKETS WILL ONLY BE ISSUED FROM LOOE AND LISKEARD STATIONS.

The Company desire to observe punctuality, and every effort will be made to ensure this.

*Traffic Manager's Office, Looe, Cornwall,
August 26th, 1902.*   HORACE H. HOLBROOK, Traffic Manager.

JOHN PHILP, MACHINE PRINTING WORKS, LISKEARD.

A scene of great tranquility, with *Lady Margaret* taking water at Looe and the ex-Mersey Railway coaches waiting at the platform.

Author's collection

belong to the Liskeard section were brought up from Looe in the rear of a goods train, which was drawn by the engine "Kilmar", the driver being Mr. R. Miller, Mr. J. Horrell acting as guard. All went well until the arrival at Liskeard soon after six, where the five carriages were uncoupled from the goods trucks. At this period the rain was falling heavily, with the result that the rails were very greasy after the prolonged dry weather. Suddenly, and before the driver could get his engine back to couple up again for shunting, the carriages were seen to be moving down the gradient. Almost before the startled officials could realise what had occurred they were beyond reach and soon out of sight round the bend, and then coming into sight again were seen rushing down the incline at great speed, and gathering way with every yard. This occurred soon after 6.15, and knowing that the 6 o'clock passenger train from Looe to Liskeard was shortly due at Coombe, information was with the utmost promptitude telephoned to the signalman at Coombe Junction, Edmund Marsh, of what had occurred, and requesting him to stop the oncoming train and open the gates. Fortunately the order was speedily obeyed, and barely had the passenger train been pulled up at the distant signal when the runaway carriages came thundering down the steep gradient at a speed which is estimated to have been at least 60 miles an hour. Fortunately, all was clear, and the carriages reached the level without mishap, rushed past the station, and ran on to Moorswater at slightly reduced speed. At Moorswater there are six sidings, one on the right leading to the engine shed and another on the left to the china clay yard, where a number of carriages were standing. The points were set for the central track leading straight to the carriage shed. This was a lightly-constructed building, some 60ft in length, built of wood on a two-feet dwarf wall with galvanised iron roof. Inside the shed were two carriages, the door being closed, whilst some

yards away from the door were two others, which are in every-day use. Into these the oncoming carriages dashed with terrific force, the first of the standing cars being completely telescoped.

'This did not stop the cars, and the debris was forced into the shed, the doors parting like paper. Cannoning into the carriages inside the shed, the latter were driven clean through the end wall of brick, and forced into the meadow beyond, keeping upright however. At the same moment the whole of the side of the shed on the near side collapsed, together with a considerable part of the iron roof.

'The roar of the impact is described by an onlooker as being like the bursting of a boiler, and many people in the district thought that that was what had occurred. The piled-up wreckage presented an extraordinary spectacle, when seen by a *Cornish Times* reporter soon after the accident. The two carriages which met in the shock are piled up one over the other, being battered out of all semblance of their former shape, the sides and flooring being practically reduced to matchwood, whilst covering them is a large portion of contorted galvanised roofing, some partially resting on the ground. Fragments of the shedding on that side are strewn along the meadow, and the whole presents a hopeless condition of wreckage. One of the few who witnessed the mishap said when the carriages were forced back in the shed the wreckage flew high in the air, and the bursting of the galvanised roofing and smashing of glass was as the noise of thunder. It would seem that for some weeks a couple of carpenters have been engaged in raising the roof of the engine shed. For some reason last evening they knocked off work at 5 o'clock. Had they been at work, such was the speed with which the carriages crossed the level that they would have been involved in the smash, and it is scarcely possible to conceive that they would have escaped with their lives. For several days also men had been

Caradon with a loaded stone train drawing away from the reversal at Crows Nest, probably in 1907. The ex-GWR brake van was acquired in 1903 and the GWR wagons in the train were probably conveying stone from Cheesewring Quarry to the major engineering works on the main line between Saltash and St. Germans.

L & GRP

engaged in painting one of the carriages in the shed, which was driven through the wall and partially wrecked.

'Fortunately the ordinary traffic was not interfered with, as the smash took place at a point a considerable distance off the main line, and no injury was done at intervening points.'

A footnote adds that the noise of the impact could clearly be heard from the GWR station at Liskeard!

This setback, which might indicate a slackness in operating practices, clearly did not affect a relationship with the GWR which was becoming increasingly cordial. On 28th February 1906 Holbrook was able to report that for the first time Liskeard and Looe Railway carriage stock had run over GWR metals on a school excursion from Looe to Doublebois. Later in the same year the GWR assented to its own rolling stock, and that of other main line companies, being worked on to the Caradon line, thus saving much transhipping. About this time the GWR was reconstructing the Cornwall main line between Saltash and St. Germans along a new alignment and large quantities of stone from the Cheesewring Quarry were used in the building work of three new viaducts across the tidal creeks at St. Germans, Nottar and Forder. This work was completed in 1908 and no doubt the use of the GWR's own wagons, and the wish to avoid transhipping of loads, was a factor in the relaxation of the Great Western's attitude to the smaller company.

The metals of the old L & C line had received some attention since 1901 when only one train per week sufficed to clear the traffic. An increase in granite traffic has already been mentioned and in 1907 a newly-formed company took a lease on the Phoenix Mine with a view to revitalizing it. Heavy equipment and plant for the new workings arrived by rail at Liskeard and was conveyed onwards over the L & C line. A 19-ton boiler arrived on a 75ft long LNWR

Track on the Liskeard and Caradon line near St. Cleer c.1907 newly relaid in anticipation of heavier traffic to and from the Phoenix United Mine. At this stage the discarded stone sleeper blocks had been left at the lineside. The sharply curved line required a continuous check rail whilst the route had also been newly fenced.   *Collection Maurice Dart*

bogie truck and a series of photographs taken at the site of the works at Phoenix clearly show that this ungainly vehicle made the journey over the lightweight metals. A large casting weighing 19 tons arrived on a six-wheeled wagon and this too made the tortuous journey over the delicate permanent way of the L & C.

One goods train, and often two ran every day at this time and usually consisted of engine, ten wagons and a 10-ton goods brake van. As well as the increase in traffic in connection with the re-opening of the Phoenix Mine, the upturn in stone traffic from the Cheesewring Quarry required an additional crane to be installed in the quarry itself and extra sidings provided outside the quarry entrance.

With the likelihood of some increased traffic over the former L & C line and the certainty of much improved revenue from the Liskeard—Looe section following the opening of the connection with the GWR, it might be considered that prospects were good. But this was not the case and financial difficulties were looming. Early in 1907 a private debenture holder called for a receiver to be appointed, interest not having been paid for the preceeding

six years. As the L & LR and the GWR were on friendly terms, the larger company was approached for help. The GWR, ever conscious of the threat from the LSWR which had its own ambitions in Cornwall and might be expected to make a play for the financially precarious L & LR, was ready to assist. It was agreed that as from 1st January 1909, the GWR would work the Liskeard and Looe Railway, paying the company a percentage of the receipts, and take over responsibility for the Liskeard and Caradon Railway. The agreement was confirmed by the Great Western, Liskeard and Looe and Liskeard and Caradon Railways Act 1909, which received Royal Assent on 25th July. With the destinies of both lines now under the control of the GWR authorities at Paddington, the highly individual Liskeard and Looe line might be considered to have become just another Great Western branch line. But the physical features of the line, with its winding course and unique connection with the main line, and the associated unusual operating procedures, ensured that it would retain a highly individual character under its new masters.

GWR 4—4—0ST No. 13 with ex-Mersey Railway coaches at Looe. The engine and carriage sheds in the background, and the ramshackle coal stage in the foreground, were needed as the timetable required the locomotive and train to be stabled overnight at the terminus.

Lens of Sutton

CHAPTER THREE

A GREAT WESTERN BRANCH LINE

THE new overseer of the Liskeard and Looe and Liskeard and Caradon lines was quick to assess its acquisitions and responsibilities for on 5th January 1909 W. H. Waister, Chief Outdoor Assistant to the GWR Locomotive Superintendent, reported to his superior, G. J. Churchward, on the condition of both lines. Waister reported that the track from Liskeard to Coombe Junction was of 'modern double (sic) line with chairs on cross sleepers' and that between Coombe Junction and Looe the line was 'formed of light Vignole rails on cross sleepers' with 'about 2 miles on granite blocks'. He further reported that there were sixteen staff employed in working the lines and that they were 'in every way satisfactory but a medical examination will be required and sight tested' — presumably to ensure that they would conform to GWR requirements. Drivers and firemen were working eleven hours per day, whilst one engine covered the passenger work, with two sets of men stationed at Looe and a further set of men at Moorswater to do the mineral work and shunting.

Waister suggested that 'for the present all arrangements might remain undisturbed' and that later all the necessary work could be done from the former Cornwall Railway carriage works at Lostwithiel and at Par, leaving only enginemen and cleaners on the Liskeard and Looe line. In due course this was done — the operating staff came into the employ of the GWR and, whilst some eventually moved away, others remained on the Looe branch for much of their often lengthy service. Horace Holbrook, the L & LR Traffic Manager, also joined the GWR and his potential was evidently noted by his new employers for by 1919 he had been promoted to the position of Chief Assistant Station Master at Paddington, a post which he retained until 1921 when he left the GWR. He then joined the Ministry of Transport, Light Railway Section, where his experience

This group of Looe station staff and the train crew posing in their GWR uniforms was staged in front of 4–4–0ST No. 13 in 1911. Bill Hocking (fourth from the left in the back row) started with the L & LR and remained as a fireman at Moorswater for many years after the GWR takeover.

L & GRP

29

4—4—0ST No. 13 drawing an up passenger train of GWR carriage stock into Sandplace station early in 1909.

Sandplace station looking towards Liskeard in 1909. Following the working agreement with the GWR, an early action was the alteration of the overline bridges between Looe and Coombe Junction, authorisation for this work being granted on 1st July 1909. This view shows the bridge in its original form. *L & GRP*

with the Liskeard and Looe Railway no doubt proved invaluable, and he remained there until 1930. A lengthy retirement in Ilfracombe followed where he resided until his death in 1958, at the age of 90 years.

Whilst the Liskeard and Looe line was functioning satisfactorily and might be expected to continue to do so, the new owners of the Caradon line looked at its acquisition with the possibility of improving its viability. There was a suggestion that the L & C line be converted to a 'light railway' to allow the introduction of a summertime passenger service and there was even consideration given to resuscitating the northward extension from Kilmar towards Alternum for which the old L & C company had obtained Parliamentary powers back in the 1880s. Fortunately for the GWR, reason prevailed and neither scheme was pursued for both would surely have been doomed to expensive failure. A more modest scheme to introduce a 'road motor' service to the area was also not proceeded with. Some improvements were made to the L & C however; sections of the line were relaid in modern bullhead rail, resting in cast-iron chairs on wooden cross sleepers and, in 1910, a new goods loop siding and goods lock-up were constructed near the 12 mile post, to serve the village of St. Cleer and surrounding area.

In March 1909 the *Railway Magazine* felt moved to comment on the GWR's working arrangement with the

Liskeard & Looe Railway and as well as reporting that the staff would wear GW uniforms — they 'seem much in need of new uniforms of some kind' remarked the writer — they also speculated on possible alterations to the connection between the GWR and the L & LR at Liskeard to permit through running and looked forward to coaches from Paddington to Looe off the down 'Limited'. In the event, the connection between the main line and the branch was not greatly altered and there has never been any through running of passenger trains to and from the Looe branch.

Immediate improvements to the Looe line included the replacement of further sections of the track with modern bullhead rail, although as late as 1911 there were still several lengths of the original flat-bottom rails in use spiked to granite blocks — surely the last example of this early form of permanent way to carry a regular service of passenger trains in this country.

In addition, the rolling stock of the old company was carefully assessed but much of it did not match up to GWR standards. *Caradon* had been scrapped in 1907, but the three surviving locomotives, *Lady Margaret, Cheesewring* and *Kilmar* were taken into Great Western stock, as were some of the Liskeard and Looe Railway coaches of more recent construction. The rest, which included all of the old Liskeard and Caradon Railway rolling stock, was in poor condition and was soon disposed of by the GWR. In 1910 the Great Western reconstructed the overline bridges between Looe and Coombe Junction ostensibly to allow the through running of coaches from the main line. In due course, GWR passenger carriages were introduced to the line but they were four- and six-wheel vehicles which, although of standard Great Western design, were no more modern than the former L & L stock they had replaced.

Traffic on the Liskeard and Looe line continued to increase after the GWR had commenced its working arrangement and Looe became firmly established as a popular holiday resort. As well as the ancient features of the old town, with the low stone slate-roofed cottages in narrow streets and alleyways, there had been much development in more recent years which had provided the

town with many hotels and boarding houses for the influx of visitors. The ever-busy harbour with its fishing fleet proved a great attraction whilst Looe was an ideal base from which to explore the surrounding area by wagonette, destinations such as Polperro and Bodinnick, for the ferry to Fowey, proving especially popular. The highly efficient GWR publicity machine was soon promoting cheap fares for special occasions which brought extra traffic to the line for events such as Looe Regatta Day, whilst, in the opposite direction, excursions were advertised from Looe and East Cornwall to national events such as football matches, race meetings, etc. Goods traffic, too, on the Looe line was substantial. The rich agricultural nature of the surrounding area was good for the railway and large quantities of

The picturesque setting of Causeland station in the 1900s.
Lens of Sutton

Causeland station in 1909.

The Phœnix United Mines, Liskeard

A postcard view of the re-established Phoenix United Mine in the 1900s. Heavy machinery for the mine was transported over the lightweight rails and stub points of the track in the foreground.
Author's collection

potatoes left the area by rail during the season, whilst on market days at Looe substantial quantities of livestock were conveyed. The fishing fleet provided a substantial traffic in herring, mackerel and pilchards and the town's ability to despatch fresh fish to London and other markets with ease meant that the traffic remained of importance to the line until the early 1950s. Coal, too, was a major traffic, for domestic consumption and for the gasworks at Looe. China clay from the dries at Moorswater remained an important traffic to Looe until 1914 but sadly there was little other mineral traffic to sustain the Caradon line. A small amount of granite traffic continued to emanate from the quarries but the promised revival of the Phoenix United Mine failed to produce results. A massive investment of capital had funded an entirely new shaft along with the attendant engine house and new engine, and the refurbishment of older shafts, but, after six years, very little ore had been extracted. A further imput of capital was required to finance exploration and to provide additional water pumping capacity, but the events of August 1914 prevented the necessary investment. Development work at the site ceased on the outbreak of war and by October 1914 most of the equipment had been brought to the surface. Thus ended the last mining operation at Caradon and with the demise of Phoenix United went the principal reason for the retention of the Liskeard and Caradon line.

A service of one train thrice-weekly continued to remove the remaining granite traffic from Caradon and equipment from Phoenix United — then being dismantled — but by 1916 the GWR could no longer justify its retention. As a result of a Government directive, from 1st January 1917, the line, along with a number of other lightly-used GWR branches, was closed to traffic as a wartime economy measure. The rails were removed soon afterwards and local

G. W. R.
CLOSING
BRANCH LINES & STATIONS
JANUARY 1st, 1917

The following Lines and Stations will be Closed.

BRANCHES CLOSED

Alcester and Bearley	Monmouth and Coleford
Titley and Eardisley	†Uxbridge (High St.) and Denham
Moorswater and Caradon	Bridport, East St., and West Bay

STATIONS AND HALTS CLOSED
WEEK DAYS AND SUNDAYS.

*Alcester	*Eardisley	Penar Junction Halt
Almeley	Great Alne	†Pontnewydd (Lower)
Bassaleg (G.W.)	Hart's Hill & Woodside	Pontrhydyrun
Berwig Halt	Ide	St. Lawrence Platform
Brampford Speke	Lightmoor Platform	†Saltney
Cheltenham (Malvern Road)	Linley	Stretton-on-Fosse
*Coleford	Llangeinor	Teigngrace
Daisy Bank	†Llangonoyd	Tidenham
Dawlish Warren	Lyonshall	†Uxbridge (High St.)
Dunstall Park	Newland	Vicarage Crossing Halt

* Closed for Great Western Trains only.   † Closed for Passenger Traffic only.

SUNDAYS.

In addition to the above, the following Stations will be closed on Sundays.

Ashburton	Colnbrook	Lustleigh	St. Ives
Bearley	Combe Junction	Marlborough	St. Keyne
Brixham	Daisy Bank	Middletown	Staines
Bovey	Dunstall Park	Moretonhampstead	Staverton
Bridport	Hanwood	Nancegollan	Stratford-on-Avon
Buckfastleigh	Heathfield	Pembridge	Titley
Buttington	Helston	Pill	Toller
Carbis Bay	Kingsland	Powerstock	Twerton-on-Avon
Causland	Kington	Portbury	Westbury (Salop)
Clevedon	Lelant	Portishead	Wilmcote
Clifton Bridge	Looe	Sandplace	Yockleton
Claverdon			

Paddington Station,
December 22nd, 1916.

FRANK POTTER, General Manager.

WYMAN & SONS, Ltd., Printers, &c., Fetter Lane, E.C.

The exposed nature of the landscape around Caradon Hill is apparent in this view of the site of the former Polwrath depot on 12th June 1934. At this point the original route to Cheesewring, via the Gonemena incline, diverged from the line to South Caradon.

L & GRP

legend has it that they were shipped to Russia; others say that they went to France — but in all certainty they were used elsewhere to aid the war effort. As an additional economy measure, the Sunday service of passenger trains on the Liskeard and Looe line was withdrawn and did not in fact reappear for many years. A reduction in the coasting traffic, due to the submarine menace in the English Channel, may have benefited the inwards goods traffic over the Looe line whilst the virtual collapse of the china clay industry in Cornwall during the Great War would have

adversely affected the railway's receipts. Otherwise there were little changes to the line during the war although, in terms of men and materials, the area made its own contribution to the grim struggle.

Although the war continued until November 1918, a number of day trippers continued to visit the area and Looe remained a popular destination for a day-out from the Plymouth area. One such visitor, who made a trip on the line as a child in the final summer of the war, recalls that two engines were in use. 4—4—0 saddle tank No. 13 was at

The disused L & CR goods shed at Minions in 1934.   *L & GRP*

View along the route of the Kilmar line, below Cheesewring Quarry, with stone sleeper blocks still in situ on 11th July 1986.   *Author*

View east through the main-line platforms at Liskeard.   *L & GRP*

Below: The Looe branch platform at Liskeard, looking toward the buffer stop in 1922.   *L & GRP*

work on the passenger service whilst an 0–6–0ST of the '1361' class, of the type normally employed in the docks at Plymouth, worked the goods service. The latter was a temporary replacement for No. 1308 *Lady Margaret* which may have been away receiving works attention.

Throughout the Great War, Britain's railways had been under Government control. In 1919 an Act of Parliament was passed which established the Ministry of Transport and provided for the Government to retain control of the railways for a further two years whilst their future was decided. The outcome of this deliberation was the Railways Act of August 1921 which required that all of the railway companies of Great Britain, with a few very minor exceptions, should be grouped into four large companies. Only the Great Western Railway survived this major upheaval intact and, as well as absorbing those lines already leased or worked, such as the Liskeard and Looe Railway, it took over a number of larger companies in Wales and elsewhere. The final duty of the directors of the Liskeard and Looe Railway was to vote themselves out of office, and on 1st January 1923 the line in its entirety passed into the control of the GWR with its affairs now conducted from the headquarters at far-away Paddington station.

Once the Great Western had assumed complete responsibility for the Liskeard and Looe line, a number of improvements were implemented to bring the branch fully up to GWR standards. Work continued on the permanent way until eventually the entire line had been relaid using standard GWR materials, consisting of bullhead rails resting in cast-iron chairs, to the best standards of the time. The signalling also was upgraded with much new equipment of GWR pattern being installed and the best of the old equipment retained and adapted using GWR materials. Facilities were improved at the stations — the platform at Liskeard

Coombe Junction on 31st May 1922. Although the GWR had taken over the L & LR on 1st January, it had already added the signal on the left which controlled access to Moorswater whilst the Saxby & Farmer starting signals had been equipped with GWR arms and lamps.

L & GRP

St. Keyne station presenting a very tidy appearance on 31st May 1922.

L & GRP

A similarly tidy appearance at Causeland and Sandplace (below) both photographed on 31st May 1922.   *L & GRP*

Looking along the platform at Looe in 1922.

L & GRP

was lengthened almost immediately — whilst all along the line the GWR made its mark upon the recently acquired property with the replacement of poster boards, notice boards, etc., of standard pattern.

The train service during this early period of full GWR ownership continued to be worked using the four- and six-wheel coaches previously employed, but the motive power was very soon improved. As early as 1918 a GWR 0—6—0 saddle tank was temporarily transferred to Moorswater shed during the summer months and these locomotives were increasingly common until they had become the norm by the time of the GWR takeover. By 1924 the first of the 'small prairie' tanks arrived and commenced an association with the line which was to last until the end of steam operation in 1961. No. 4400 was the first to

arrive whilst the first '45XX' arrived in 1926, the larger tank '4575' class making its debut in 1927.

Four- and six-wheel coaches continued in use until around 1930 when they were replaced by wooden panelled bogie coaches which had been built in the last few years of the nineteenth century. These remained in use until 1934 when brand-new steel panelled bogie coaches arrived from Swindon Works where they had been built. Like the '45XX' class engines, similar vehicles remained in use until the end of steam operations.

1923 proved to be a high point in the fortunes of the Liskeard and Looe branch for by the mid-1920s the Great Western was facing increasing competition from road traffic and the company was considering ways in which economies might be made in the working of its branch lines. Statistics

'850' class 0—6—0ST No. 1941 with the branch train at Looe on 10th July 1924.
H. C. Casserley

No. 1941 again, this time shunting a 'Python' motor car van along Looe quay, on 10th July 1924.
H. C. Casserley

H. C. Casserley

'850' class 0—6—0PT No. 1973 engaged in shunting at Looe on 10th July 1924.

for the traffic dealt with at Looe in 1923, the first full year of GWR ownership, reveal that ten staff were employed at the terminus and the receipts totalled £25,054 broken down as follows: passenger £6,116, parcels £10,821, and goods £9,200, whilst 148 wagons of livestock were forwarded and received.

In 1925 a survey of the company's branch lines was made and the figures for Looe revealed some interesting statistics. Receipts from Looe station totalled £21,502 broken down thus: passenger £6,417, parcels £6,904, goods £8,181, which compared with the 1924 total of £21,771. The passenger traffic was worked by a down service of seven passenger trains and one mixed train with 'eight' up passenger trains. Goods traffic was worked by one train in each direction. Goods tonnage forwarded and received in 1925 consisted of coal and minerals 5,841 and general goods 6,644, the principal traffic consisting of grain and manure. In addition, 3,512 cans of milk left the area by rail

44XX 2–6–2T No. 4410 arrived at Moorswater shed in February 1925 and is seen here entering Liskeard station on 1st July 1926 with a train from Looe. *Author's collection*

No. 4400 was the first 'small Prairie' to work on the line, arriving in November 1924. This view was taken in 1925 and shows her shunting 'Bloater' fish vans on the quay at Looe.

D. B. Hart

A livestock market was regularly held in Looe and on occasions special trains of cattle wagons were worked over the line. One such train is seen here being shunted at Looe in the mid-1920s. According to records for 1918, the empty cattle wagons left Liskeard at 11.15 a.m., arriving at Looe at 11.50 a.m. The loaded train, which was timetabled to 'run as required', left Looe at 4.20 p.m. and arrived at Liskeard at 5.02 p.m.

and 176 trucks of livestock were conveyed by goods train. It was proposed that savings in maintenance and staff might be made if the train service was reduced or rearranged to permit the removal of the electric train tablet system of single-line working. In practice it was found that the level of traffic made any reduction in the service impossible and

the electric train tablet system continued in use until beyond the end of steam in the 1960s.

One of the factors causing the steady decline in passenger numbers was the introduction of motor bus services to the area in the early 1920s. The first operator was Devon Motor Transport Co. which ran buses on two routes from Liskeard

45XX 2–6–2T No. 4515 on a down passenger train near Steps Lodge in 1928. The fence visible in the background was created to prevent trains from alarming horses on the adjacent road.

D. B. Hart

An unidentified 'small Prairie' with an up passenger train near Steps Lodge.

Collection Robert Tivendale

Arriving passengers making their way from the station towards the town in the late 1920s. In the background the locomotive can be seen shunting the passenger stock in preparation for the return journey.   *Collection Paul Karau*

Local proprietor Albert West's 20-seater charabanc proudly displayed on Buller Quay in the 1920s. Such vehicles ran excursions for visitors who arrived in the district by train. The rails of the Quay line may be seen to the right of the vehicle.   *Author's collection*

The beach at Looe in the early 1930s. *Author's collection*

to Looe via Duloe, and less frequently via Morval. A lengthy service also ran from Torpoint to Looe via Downderry and Hessenford. In 1928 the company was taken over by the National Omnibus and Transport Co. which, in turn, formed a major constituent of the newly-formed Western National Omnibus Co. in 1929.

From the depot at Bay Tree Hill, Liskeard, the bus service to Looe, route No. 69, ran via the GWR station, Duloe, East Looe, where it conveniently stopped at the bridge, and terminated on the quayside at West Looe. Service No. 70 ran less frequently via Morval and similarly paused at the bridge in East Looe before terminating at West Looe. The service from Torpoint to Looe originally ran through to Polperro but this last portion of the journey was passed over to Pearce Brothers, local operators, in September 1931. The Torpoint–Looe service had the route number 78A. By the summer of 1935, service No. 69 had four journeys each way per day, service No. 70 had two journeys each way per day, whilst service 78A operated eight journeys each way per day.

Although the motor vehicle was beginning to make its presence felt by the 1920s, the line continued to make an important contribution to the prosperity of the area, especially in the summer months. As well as transporting arriving and departing holidaymakers at the beginning and end of their stay in the area, the railway played an important part in the enjoyment of their holiday. Specially arranged excursions were widely advertised and some of the most popular were trips by GWR steamers on Wednesdays and Saturdays from Millbay Docks, Plymouth to Looe. The steamers were *Sir Francis Drake* and *Sir Walter Raleigh*,

Postcard view of 'old Looe'. *Author's collection*

EAST LOOE. 4613.

A general view of East Looe from West Looe in the 1920s, showing the GWR goods yard to the north of Looe Bridge and Buller Quay to the south.

Author's collection

This view, taken on a damp, dull day in 1924, shows No. 4405 drawing a train of wagons along the Quay line near the end of Looe bridge immediately before entering the goods yard.
Collection P. Q. Treloar

Low tide at Looe.

Author's collection

West Looe in the 1930s.
Author's collection

No. 4515 on the quay alongside Looe fish market in 1928 with fishing nets laid out to dry in the foreground.

D. B. Hart

An undated view of East Looe apparently showing china clay wagons on the Quay line. *Collection Robert Tivendale*

Masts and spars in Looe Harbour. The derrick on the quay had been provided to load stone from Cheesewring Quarry but was disused by the 1920s. *Author's collection*

GREAT WESTERN RAILWAY

LOOE
SOUTH CORNWALL
FOR IDEAL
HOMES AND HOLIDAYS
FOR GUIDE APPLY : TOWN CLERK

Printed in England by The Campfield Press

Looking across Looe station towards West Looe in the early 1930s.

Collection Robert Tivendale

joined in the 1930s by *Sir John Hawkins* and *Sir Richard Grenville*. All were primarily employed as tenders at Millbay Docks to land passengers and mail from incoming ocean liners. Sailing time from Plymouth was around one hour and there was the option to make the return journey by rail, a popular alternative when things were rough at sea! The steamers often conveyed upwards of 800 passengers and were too large to enter the harbour at Looe. When a steamer arrived off the harbour entrance, a flotilla of boatmen, who normally worked a ferry service across the harbour between West and East Looe, would bring the passengers ashore in relays and later carry them back. For those who chose to return to Plymouth by the GWR vessel, the arrival was timed so that it steamed up Plymouth Sound at dusk just as the lights of the city were coming on, a gesture always appreciated by the passengers. Such excursions also sailed from Looe to the Eddystone Lighthouse and remained a popular local attraction until the late 1950s.

The Liskeard and Looe branch was also included as part of the holiday season ticket scheme whereby holidaymakers

could purchase a weekly ticket giving them unlimited travel by rail within a specified area. Looe fell within an area where the tickets were administered jointly by the GWR and the Southern Railway. Destinations within the area included Fowey, Bodmin, Plymouth, Princetown, Tavistock, Turnchapel, Bere Alston, Callington and Okehampton, all for a third class fare of 13s 3d in the late 1930s.

By the late 1920s, the quay line at Looe was used only for fish traffic. Granite traffic from Caradon, of course, was entirely moribund and all the china clay traffic from Moorswater now left the area by rail to Liskeard and then to Fowey docks for shipment.

As part of the terms for the absorption of the former L & LR, the GWR assumed responsibility for the maintenance of the old canal. Although it was derelict above Sandplace, the section from Sandplace to Terras was apparently still maintained in a navigable condition. Whether it was or not is open to conjecture but an employee in the GWR Plymouth District offices recalls that every month in the late 1920s they dutifully received from Looe a 'nil return' for traffic on the canal.

In 1931 the GWR legally abandoned the former Liskeard and Caradon line as part of the GWR's Act for that year. The closure and removal of track in 1917 had been intended as a temporary wartime expedient, and although there were some hopes after the war that the track might be reinstated, it was not and the former railway was left to slumber in peace on the remote moors. Periodically, agreements were reached with adjacent landowners who occasionally required to use the disused formation. For example, one such agreement was made in 1926 when the Duchy of Cornwall removed timber from the woods surrounding the course of the former L & C at High Wood north of Moorswater, motor lorries and horse and cart being permitted access via the old line from the main road at Looe Mills.

Looking along the Looe branch platform at Liskeard on 8th May 1936.   *M. F. Yarwood*

Ready to depart for Looe in the early 1930s.   *G. N. Southerden*

The view from Lodge Hill bridge on 27th August 1936 with an up train from Looe approaching Coombe Junction. *R. K. Cope*

Below: Coombe Junction, looking south in 1932 with the Liskeard line climbing away to the left and the Looe line dropping away to the right. *G. N. Southerden*

View north from the platform at Coombe Junction c.1930 with Moorswater viaduct dominating the scene in the distance.

G. N. Southerden

This c.1930 snapshot was taken looking south from a train standing at the platform at Coombe Junction before the engine had run round its train.

G. N. Southerden

Running round at Coombe Junction in 1933. *R. W. Kidner*

Looking north at Coombe Junction with the engine emerging from the headshunt to run round its train.

The view from Lamellion bridge c.1930 with a train departing from Coombe Junction.

G. N. Southerden

Looking north from Lamellion bridge towards Moorswater c.1930.   *G. N. Southerden*

Moorswater engine shed in April 1936 with both locomotives about their duties.
          W. A. Camwell

'4575' class 2—6—2T No. 5501 shunting wagons at Moorswater in the early 1930s.   *Lens of Sutton*

St. Keyne on 27th August 1936 with an old lime kiln visible beyond the station.
R. K. Cope

By the early 1930s, summer passenger services on the Liskeard and Looe line were dealt with by eight trains per day, which was increased by two extra evening services on Saturdays only. The country was just emerging from recession and in the summer months of 1933 extra trains were run on weekdays and a Sunday service was reinstated. This seasonal increase in the service remains a feature of the line to this day. In spite of this increase in services, throughout the decade receipts maintained a steady decline. In 1930, 47,197 tickets were issued at Looe and total receipts amounted to £20,268. By 1938, the last year for which full figures are available for the GWR period of ownership, the totals had declined to 22,110 tickets issued, with receipts amounting to £14,825. It should be borne in mind that these figures represent a decline in local traffic rather than holiday visitors who purchased their tickets at the point of departure of their journey.

Throughout the inter-war period, there was a gradual move towards paid holidays, with one and a half million manual workers benefiting from them in 1925 and four million by 1937. 1938 brought the Holidays with Pay Act which ensured that many families could enjoy at least one week's holiday at the seaside, although the Act was not fully implemented until after the Second World War. Resorts such as Looe could only benefit from these new-found freedoms but the outbreak of the war meant that it was to be a number of years before the effects were fully felt.

— This picture of No. 4578, taken near Plashford bridge in 1929, shows a 'Bloater' fish van being conveyed as the first vehicle in an up train.
D. B. Hart

An up passenger train pausing at Causeland on 12th June 1934. The first vehicle in the train, a van, was almost certainly conveying 'passengers luggage in advance'. Surviving records are rare but in 1937, for example, the London PLA van was conveyed on Saturdays by the 4.00 p.m. Looe to Liskeard train, transferring at Liskeard to the 2.20 p.m. ex Penzance to Crewe Perishables train and again at Tavistock Junction to the 4.25 p.m. ex Penzance to Paddington Perishables train.

L & GRP

Looking towards Liskeard at Sandplace station in the late 1920s.

Lens of Sutton

No. 4515 on a down train at Sandplace in 1928.

D. B. Hart

As always, the GWR actively promoted the Cornish resorts in its own holiday guide and the entry for Looe in *Holiday Haunts* for 1939 paints an appealing picture:

'In the twin towns of East and West Looe the holidaymaker can enjoy all the pleasures of a country holiday without sacrificing any of the joys of the sea-side. The towns are terraced on the wooded shores of the Looe river, which winds its way down to a tiny harbour beside the sea, and have some quaint cobbled streets and gabled houses hidden behind their pretty modern villas, for, although progressive, the citizens of Looe cherish such links with their once stirring history as remain to them, including the grand old Guildhall and the ancient Meat Market, which are the pride of East Looe, and the fine church and quaint "Jolly Sailor" Inn of West Looe.

'It is from the tops of the hills guarding the river that the true glory of Looe's situation can be best appreciated, and the ramifications of the Looe Waters traced. Then it is realised there are two rivers, with all their possibilities for fishing, boating and yachting, and the delight of innumerable walks along their banks, whilst the sea-shore, which is well sheltered by its encircling cliffs and Looe Island affords opportunities for sea-and-sun-bathing, fishing, yachting, boating, water-polo, prawning, and for motor-launch trips to the coast towns and villages of South Devon and Cornwall.'

Although the Liskeard and Looe branch paid its way throughout the inter-war period, despite the decline of some of its vital goods traffic and the loss of local passenger traffic to the alternative road transport, the GWR

THE VILLAGE, SANDPLACE.

3329.

This curve in the line, with the former canal in the foreground, is to the south of Sandplace, two miles from Looe station.

continued looking for means of making economies in the operation of the line. In 1931 the introduction of the 'Motor-Economic' System of Maintenance allowed gangs of 'platelayers' total occupation of the section of line on which they were working. This did away with the requirement for flagmen to be posted in advance of the place of work, in both directions in the case of a single line such as the Looe branch, whilst the provision of motor-trolleys allowed the number of men to be reduced. The branch was henceforth maintained by one gang based at Coombe Junction where the motor trolley and its trailer was kept. The line was divided into nine sections under the control of key boxes where the ganger could insert an occupation key to obtain possession of the section of line to be worked

Looe station in the late 1920s.   *L & GRP*

No. 4405 at Looe shortly after arrival from Liskeard during 1928.   *D. B. Hart*

Looking south from the platform at Looe c.1930 with shunting in progress in the yard.

G. N. Southerden

A general view of Looe station in April 1936.

W. A. Camwell

A passenger train awaiting departure from Looe in April 1936 whilst No. 4526 was shunting the yard. During the late 1930s there was an exception to the exclusivity of Moorswater crews in working the branch services. The daily goods train was worked by St. Blazey men who used the engine of the Laira goods to work a round trip over the line, serving Moorswater and Looe.

W. A. Camwell

on. Run-offs were also provided at each key box so that the motor-trolley could, with the aid of its own built-in turntable, be removed from the running line, to allow trains to pass.

With the country in the grip of economic recession, in 1929 the Labour Government of the day sought ways to relieve the high figures of unemployment. One answer was the Great Western Railway (Additional Powers) Act of 1936, it was proposed to build an entirely new line to Looe, diverging from the Cornwall main line at Trerule, west of St. Germans, and serving the village of Hessenford en route, with halts also at Seaton and Millendreath. Such a line would have had a profound effect on the development of Looe, the new line bringing the twin towns within

No. 4405 shunting at Looe on 23rd May 1935.

H. C. Casserley

the Loans and Guarantees Act (1929) whereby the Government would guarantee and pay the interest for several years on the capital expended on development programmes. Thus encouraged, the GWR proposed a major programme of reconstruction at important centres such as Paddington, Bristol and Cardiff and at other locations throughout the system. However, the recession continued into the 1930s and during 1936 capital from the Loan Act was used to improve the layout at Liskeard where the curve between the main line and the Looe branch was adapted to allow the use of heavier engines, and new sidings were provided. Henceforth '57XX' 0—6—0 pannier tanks were permitted to enter the yard, but the Looe branch remained restricted to uncoloured engines and '45XX' 2—6—2Ts only, beyond a stop board at the outer limit of the Looe branch station at Liskeard.

These same Government guarantees to the GWR would have had an even greater impact on Looe had a scheme, implemented in the mid-1930s, come to fruition. Under

thirty-five minutes of Plymouth and surely making them a dormitory of the city, but the uncertain international situation of the late 1930s, followed by the Second World War, ensured that the scheme did not flourish. It would most certainly have meant the end of the awkward-to-operate line from Liskeard to Looe, but, in the event, the old line survived.

By 1939 it was apparent that the new line to Looe was going to be delayed for some time, and so much-needed improvements were carried out to the existing station building at Looe which was considerably altered and extended to provide enlarged goods and parcels accommodation. These modifications were completed in time for the summer season of that year and, as events were to prove, these improvements were the last to be carried out by the GWR. As the Liskeard and Looe branch, and indeed the whole country, prepared itself again for war, it is perhaps a convenient point at which to break the narrative and look at the physical features of the line.

An Edwardian view of Liskeard station with a 4—4—0 'Bulldog' arriving with an up train. The signal box on the platform opened in 1892 and remained in use until 3rd June 1915 when the present signal box at the east end of the station was brought into use.

Photomatic

CHAPTER FOUR

ALONG THE LINE
LISKEARD: MAIN LINE STATION

ALTHOUGH the Liskeard and Caradon Railway was the first to be built in the vicinity of the town, its primary function was to convey minerals from the quarries on the moors to the Liskeard and Looe Union canal basin at Moorswater. Other than increasing the general prosperity of the area, it had little immediate effect on the development of Liskeard and it was not until 1859, when the broad gauge Cornwall Railway opened, that there was direct railway connection with the outside world

Once the Bill had received Royal Assent, construction of the Cornwall Railway progressed in a desultory manner due to the difficulties in raising finance. By 1852 the 22 miles of line between St. Austell and Liskeard were complete, but it was not until the following year that contracts were let for the construction of the line eastwards to Saltash. At the end of February 1859 the line was largely complete between Truro and St. Germans whilst at Saltash the Tamar bridge was approaching completion. On 11th April 1859 the first through train ran from Plymouth to Truro, passing Liskeard en route, and the line was approved by the Board of Trade shortly afterwards. The railway was officially opened by Prince Albert, the Prince Consort, on 2nd May, the same occasion that he inspected and named the bridge at Saltash, and the line was formally opened to traffic the following day. The first passenger train from Plymouth left for Truro at 10 a.m. and consisted of 14 carriages drawn by two engines conveying about 800 persons. It stopped for a few minutes at Liskeard and was the first public passenger train to call at the town. It was not until Wednesday, 4th May 1859, that the Cornwall Railway was fully opened for public traffic.

As first constructed, the route consisted of a single line of broad gauge rails laid in a similar manner to that used on the GWR, Bristol & Exeter and South Devon railways. Bridge rails were used, laid on longitudinal sleepers and spaced by timber transoms. Some flange rail (flatbottom) laid on cross sleepers was used in a number of sidings.

Approaching from the east, the line reached a summit about halfway between Menheniot and Liskeard at the 263 mile post.* From there the line descended at 1 in 79, crossing several narrow valleys on viaducts. Carthuther viaduct was 137 yards long and 89ft in height whilst the structure at Bolitho, named after a nearby hamlet and 182 yards long and 113 feet high, was within sight of Liskeard station. The single line then climbed for a short distance at 1 in 79, crossing the Liskeard viaduct en route, before arriving at the station. All three viaducts were constructed of timber in the well-known style employed by Brunel throughout Cornwall and elsewhere in the West Country.

A loop through the station allowed up and down trains to pass, the two platforms being provided with waiting shelters, or 'alcoves' in the parlance of the time. The platforms, and much of the goods yard, were sited in a cutting spanned by a lofty stone arch bridge which carried the main road south from the town towards Looe. The main station building, providing accommodation for the booking office, station master's office, parcels office, ladies room and waiting room, was situated at road level, above the up platform, with the main entrance facing along the road in the direction of the town, whilst the obligatory Station Hotel was situated across the road. The station building, with low gable ends, overhanging roof and tall chimneys, was of a style used by Brunel for most of the smaller Cornwall Railway stations, but over the years it has been extended and altered from its original form.

At the east of the station, on the down side of the line, was a single-road locomotive shed with coal store and an additional siding to which access was by means of a small engine turntable. Also at the east end on the up side of the line, was a siding, trailing from the down line, which allowed access via a wagon turntable to private sidings, known as 'Isaac's siding'. The main goods yard was situated to the west of the station on the up side, the two sidings serving a loading bank, cattle pens and a typical large 'Brunelian' timber goods shed.

To the west of the station, the line reverted to single track before commencing a sharp descent of ½ mile at 1 in 59 towards the viaduct at Moorswater. At a height of 147ft, this viaduct, one of the highest in Cornwall, spanned the valley of the Looe river and, at the time of opening of the Cornwall Railway, the Liskeard and Looe Railway under construction beneath. At 318 yards, Moorswater was also one of the longest in Cornwall and, leaving the viaduct, the line commenced an almost continuous climb at an average gradient of 1 in 70 to the summit of the Cornwall Railway at Doublebois.

The first major development of the Cornwall Railway line in the vicinity of Liskeard was the reconstruction of the Moorswater viaduct, as already related elsewhere. This magnificent new masonry structure was built alongside the timber viaduct it was to replace, and the work took place during 1880-81, being completed and brought into use on 25th February 1881. With an eye to the future, the new structure was built to accommodate double standard-gauge tracks although initially only a single broad-gauge track was laid. Most of the stone piers of the original timber viaduct were left standing alongside the new structure where they largely remain to this day.

*263 miles measured from London Paddington via Bristol and the reversal at Plymouth Millbay.

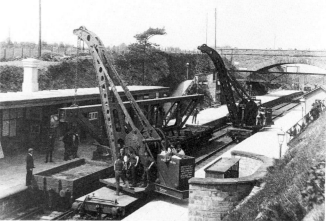

Left: Liskeard viaduct in 1893 with the original Brunel stone piers raised in brick but with the timber 'fan' supports still in place. *Right:* One of the steel lattice girders lifted by two travelling cranes in Liskeard station before being towed onto the viaduct.   *A. Leaman*

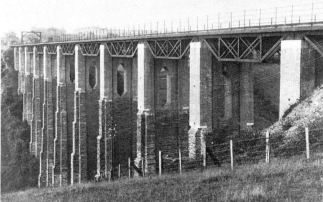

Left: Lowering the new girder into position. Apart from Sunday occupation, this gradual reconstruction of the viaduct was achieved while the normal traffic continued to cross. *Right:* The reconstructed viaduct completed in 1894 with all traces of the Brunel timber structure removed.

A. Leaman

Liskeard viaduct from the south on 29th May 1922.   *L & GRP*

A new signal box at Liskeard was brought into operation during 1892. Containing a frame of 21 levers and with a floor area of 20ft 9in x 12ft, the structure had been ordered from the Reading signal works in January 1892. It generally followed the GWR standard design of the period, but, due to the narrowness of the up platform where it was sited, the operating floor overhung the lower locking room at the front of the building. There was also a 2-lever ground frame at the east of the station controlling entry to Isaac's sidings.

Following the removal of the broad gauge in Devon and Cornwall, major engineering works were undertaken to upgrade the main line through the West Country. To the west of Liskeard the line was doubled as far as Doublebois, the second track being brought into use on 4th February 1894. The new line, which was the down line, was laid alongside the old single line and crossed the East Looe river valley by the Moorswater viaduct, which had, of course, already been rebuilt to accommodate double standard-gauge tracks nearly thirteen years earlier. To the east of Liskeard, however, the old Brunel single-track timber viaduct remained in use, although in 1894 work commenced on a replacement. Unlike Moorswater, which was replaced by an entirely new masonry structure built alongside the old timber viaduct, it was proposed to raise the stone piers of the Liskeard viaduct in brickwork to carry new wrought-iron girder spans. Once the piers had been sufficiently raised, they were capped by granite bed-stones upon which the girders were to rest. Pockets were left in the brickwork for the timber struts of the original viaduct. The girders, which, in the event, were of lattice steel construction, were brought to Liskeard station yard by rail, from where they were taken, carried by two hand cranes and drawn by a locomotive, to the required position on the viaduct, where they were lowered onto the granite bed-stones. With the girders in place, the floor was then temporarily supported so that the timber struts could be withdrawn and the structure completed. This work was undertaken in stages, from east to west, whilst throughout the operation, except for Sunday occupation, trains continued to cross the viaduct. The work on the viaduct was completed in 1894 and the line doubled eastwards to Treviddo in 1896.

Also in 1894 a new water tank and water column were erected at the west end of the down platform. The GWR minutes specify that a tank and column made for use at Brent station in South Devon 'should instead be erected at Liskeard'.

In 1895 the Bill was passed for the construction of the Liskeard and Looe Extension Railway from Coombe to Liskeard, although work did not commence for several years. Construction started in 1898, and in 1899 the General Manager of the GWR was able to report to the Traffic Committee that the L & LR had obtained powers to 'construct certain railways terminating by a junction with one of this company's goods sidings at Liskeard'. It was further proposed that 'telephonic communication' should be provided between the signal boxes of both companies.

Construction of the connecting line was largely complete by early 1901 and on 25th February the L & LR was able to inform the Board of Trade that 'the GWR have made the connection with our No. 2 line and connected the points and catch points with their main signal box'. Goods traffic may have worked over the new line to Coombe Junction almost immediately but the exchange sidings were not fully brought into use until 8th May. Passenger services started running on 15th May following the BoT inspection.

Access to the L & LR yard was by a trailing connection from the down running line via a slip which was also used as a crossover between the up and down main lines. Two sidings, which had been in existence prior to the construction of the L & LR, were left in situ, and access to the new yard was by a sharp curve of 5 chains radius. There were four sidings used for the exchange of traffic between the two companies. The most easterly was for the reception of all traffic from the GWR to the L & LR, including coal, etc, for Isaac's stores, now served by a siding off the L & LR. The second road was for the reception of all traffic from the L & LR to the GWR, whilst the third was the L & LR's through goods line which was used for running round locomotives, etc., and there were instructions that no traffic was to stand on it or foul it. The fourth siding was for the use of the GWR for loading and unloading traffic.

Entry to the exchange sidings from the GWR was under the control of the Liskeard signal box, and a ground frame operating a catch point, which protected the GWR running lines, was bolted from the GWR 'box. Exit at the further end of the exchange sidings, to the shunting spur and to the L & LR running lines, was under the control of the L & LR signal box.

Strict instructions regarding the method by which traffic between the two companies was to be worked were issued by the GWR Divisional Offices at Plymouth. No operation between the two companies was allowed until the words 'Traffic may pass' had been given by telephone between the GWR and L & LR signal boxes, and a complete record of all movements between the two companies had to be maintained. In June 1901, the GWR approved an agreement with the L & LR under which, in consideration of payment by the L & LR of £25 per annum, traffic to and from their system would be dealt with by the Railway Clearing House, as GWR traffic. In 1903 the GWR permitted the L & LR Company to erect a noticeboard on posts at the back of the fence adjoining the gate to the approach road of the GWR station, directing potential passengers 'To The Liskeard and Looe Station'.

By the turn of the century, communication between East Cornwall and the outside world was further improved when exchange apparatus was provided for use by the up and down 'Travelling Post Office' trains. Sited at the west of the GWR Liskeard station, access for GPO staff was by lineside footpath from a lane which passed beneath the main line by an accommodation bridge. The down London Mail and the up North Mail both used the apparatus, which remained in daily use until the early 1960s.

Further improvements and alterations to the GWR station included the lengthening of the down platform by 200ft at the Penzance end during 1907 and, in 1909, the removal of the small 23ft 6in diameter engine turntable, which was worn out and beyond repair. In 1915 a new signal box was provided and was brought into use on 3rd June. It was sited at the east end of the down platform and contained a frame of 36 levers in an operating floor measuring 29ft x 12ft 8in. As well as taking over the function of the earlier signal box, it also replaced the ground frame which controlled access to the 'Looe' yard, thus fulfilling a BoT siting requirement made years before, but not enforced, when the 1894 signal box was opened. Constructed entirely of timber, with a hipped slate-covered roof to the standard GWR design of the period, it remains in use to this day. Gongs were provided for communication between the signal box and staff on the ground in the 'Looe' yard, the code in use being: one long beat — clear main line; two beats — main line is right to come out of Looe line sidings.

By 1918 the small GWR locomotive shed at Liskeard had been closed. Indeed it had been used only as a service point since October 1912 when the last engine allocation was recorded. The structure, of stone with a gabled slate roof and measuring 38ft by 10ft 6in, was subsequently demolished.

The 1920s saw further alterations to the facilities at Liskeard. Once the L & LR was firmly under the wing of the GWR, the 'Looe' yard was remodelled in 1925. In 1926 the lattice steel girders of the Liskeard viaduct were replaced by wrought-iron girders, the original ones suffering from extensive corrosion. In connection with this work, the engineers department installed sidings to the east of the station on the site formerly occupied by the locomotive shed, and when the reconstruction work on the viaduct was completed, it was decided to retain them for traffic purposes. Wagons of china clay from the 'dries' at Moorswater would be brought up by the Looe branch locomotive and left in these sidings for collection by passing westbound goods trains for onward movement to Lostwithiel and Fowey for shipment. In addition, ballast wagons from Clicker Tor quarry at Menheniot, to the east of Liskeard,

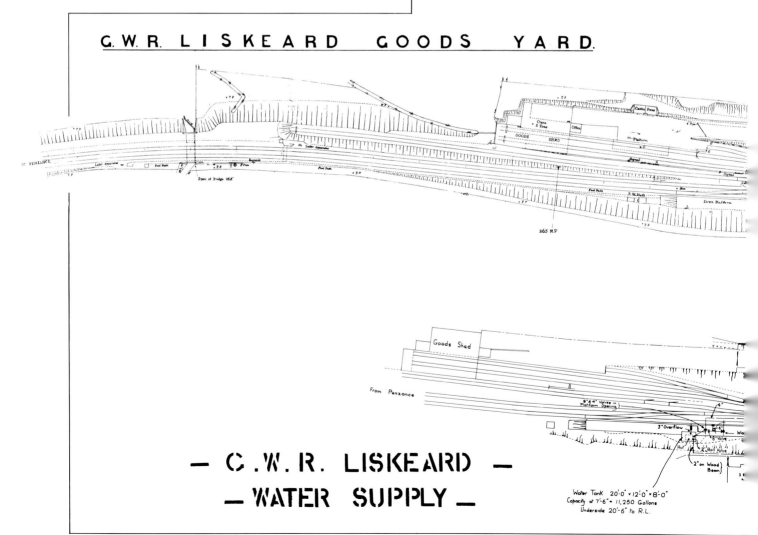

G.W.R. LISKEARD GOODS YARD.

— G.W.R. LISKEARD —
— WATER SUPPLY —

Water Tank 20'-0" x 12'-0" x 8'-0"
Capacity at 7'-6" = 11,250 Gallons
Underside 20'-6" to R.L.

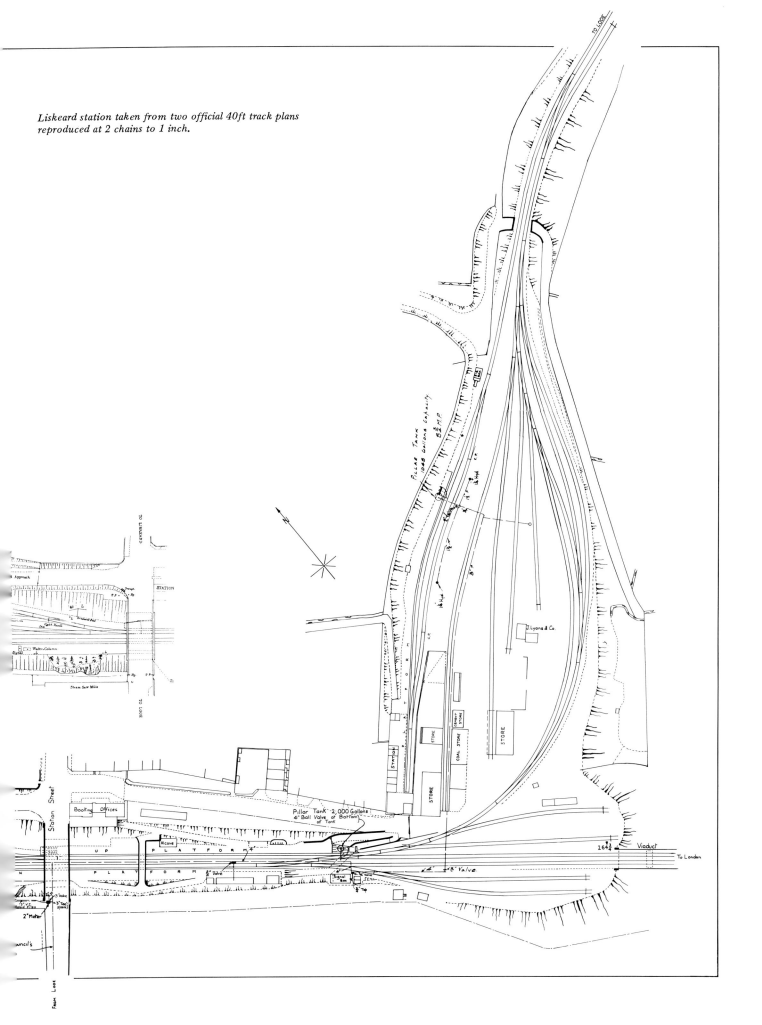

Liskeard station taken from two official 40ft track plans
reproduced at 2 chains to 1 inch.

could be accommodated here when required. Due to the previous use of the site, these sidings were known to railwaymen as the 'engine shed sidings'.

Further work, under the Government Guaranteed Loans Scheme, was carried out in 1936, when the curve through the 'Looe' yard was adapted to allow heavier locomotives — in particular '57XX' 0–6–0PTs — into the yard. At the same time, the junction with the main line was remodelled. Access to the main line from the branch remained via a trailing connection to the down line but the slip, which had also served as a crossover between the two main running

lines, was done away with and replaced by a new crossover slightly to the east, nearer to the Liskeard viaduct. The new works were brought into use in February 1937. No other alterations are recorded prior to the Second World War and it was not until peace had returned to Europe that any further improvements were made at this Cornish junction station.

During 1947, the last year of Great Western Railway ownership, an additional waiting room was provided on the down platform whilst the old 'Brunelian' alcove on the up platform was converted to a waiting room. Both rooms

An exterior view of the ex-Cornwall Railway station building at Liskeard. The canopy has been removed in recent years.
Collection Paul Karau

This grounded coach was formerly a GWR sleeping car and was used as the Staff Association clubroom. Photographed in August 1963, it has been removed in recent years.
P. J. Garland

This view across the deep cutting in which the station is situated, shows the enclosed circulating area by the station building and the old GWR sleeping car body.

P. J. Garland

An unidentified 'Hall' class entering Liskeard with an up passenger train in the early 1930s. The poster hoarding on the right marks the site of the 1892 signal box which was replaced in 1915.

D. B. Hart

were heated and lit by gas which was also used for platform lighting. It is probable that the strictly utilitarian enclosure of the circulating area beside the main station building at the top of the ramp leading to the up platform, was carried out at this time, but this has not been confirmed.

One of the last acts of the GWR was the recruitment, in 1947, of additional staff at Liskeard. An extra porter and an extra shunter were required due to the introduction of the 44-hour working week. The two men transferred from Doublebois and Menheniot stations and commenced their new duties in the early months of 1948.

Nationalisation brought few immediate changes to Britain's railways but in due course new uniforms, paper-work, locomotive and rolling stock liveries, brought the

63XX 2–6–0 No. 6397 approaching Liskeard on an up 'F' class freight train in the late 1950s. *Collection R. S. Carpenter*

This view, taken in the late 1900s, provides a glimpse of the goods yard at the west end of Liskeard station. *Liskeard Old Cornwall Society*

Looking west from the footbridge at Liskeard circa 1948-49, clearly showing the up refuge alongside the goods yard and the 1907 extension of the down platform.
J. H. Moss

0—6—0PT No. 4656 waiting in the up refuge siding at Liskeard with a goods train on 11th August 1951.
H. F. Wheeller

stamp of the state-run system to Cornwall. Staff at Liskeard station coped with the immense growth in postwar holiday traffic as people indulged themselves in the seaside holidays that they had been denied during the conflict. In the years following the war, before the large-scale transfer of holiday traffic to the roads, the Western Region of British Railways handled vast numbers of holidaymakers during the summer months. To make the lot of the railway-

men at Liskeard a little easier, a four-wheeled electrically-powered truck was provided in time for the summer season of 1952. It was used for transferring passengers' luggage from the main line station to the 'Looe' branch station, and when not in use was accommodated in a wooden hut adjacent to the Looe branch station building. The battery-charging equipment was also housed in the hut and the truck would be recharged overnight. Goods traffic, too,

Looking east towards Plymouth in August 1948 with an up passenger train at the platform. *D. Clayton*

'Hall' class 4—6—0 No. 4940 *Ludford Hall* running light engine through Liskeard station on 11th August 1951. This view shows the ramp from the up platform to the station building at the top of the cutting.   *H. F. Wheeller*

This view from the footbridge, looking east in 1948 or 1949, clearly shows the connection to the Looe branch. The sidings where the locomotive can be seen shunting wagons were known as the 'engine shed' sidings, whilst the remainder of its train can be seen on the down main line.

J. H. Moss

'Hall' class No. 5940 *Whitbourne Hall* entering Liskeard with a down 'F' class freight in 1947.

Cty. Xpress Publishing

continued to be healthy throughout the 1950s and, in the 'Looe' yard, pre-cast concrete traders stores were provided, and then extended, even as late as 1960.

The 1960s, however, brought many changes caused by the end of steam traction and the general reduction in services. In the 'Looe' yard the introduction of diesel multiple units in 1961 and the withdrawal of branch goods services, except for clay traffic from Moorswater, in 1963 meant that the trackwork in the yard was severely rationalised. At the west of the 'main line' station, the sidings,

goods shed and cattle dock have all been removed, and at the time of writing, the site is waste ground.

However, Liskeard station remains open to passengers as the Looe branch survives and there is a healthy commuter traffic to Plymouth. The old Cornwall Railway station building is still in use, and is staffed, whilst the signal box of 1915 remains in use, controlling access to the branch and maintaining a small outpost of mechanical signalling in the Great Western tradition.

No. 4569 leaving the Looe branch yard and crossing the up main to join the down main line.
Hugh Davies

A quiet interlude at Liskeard in August 1963. The small wooden hut between the fence and the station building housed the 'Electruk' platform barrow and associated battery charging equipment.
P. J. Garland

A view in the late 1950s across the Liskeard Valley, showing the seemingly precarious situation of the Looe branch yard.

Collection R. S. Carpenter

Self-explanatory notice-board at the entrance to the Looe branch yard at Liskeard in June 1948. This board was still in position in July 1966 when the author first visited the line, five years after steam had ceased. The old carriage body on the right was provided as storage accommodation for cattle feed awaiting distribution by Lever Bros. It was later replaced by a pre-cast concrete structure.

D. Clayton

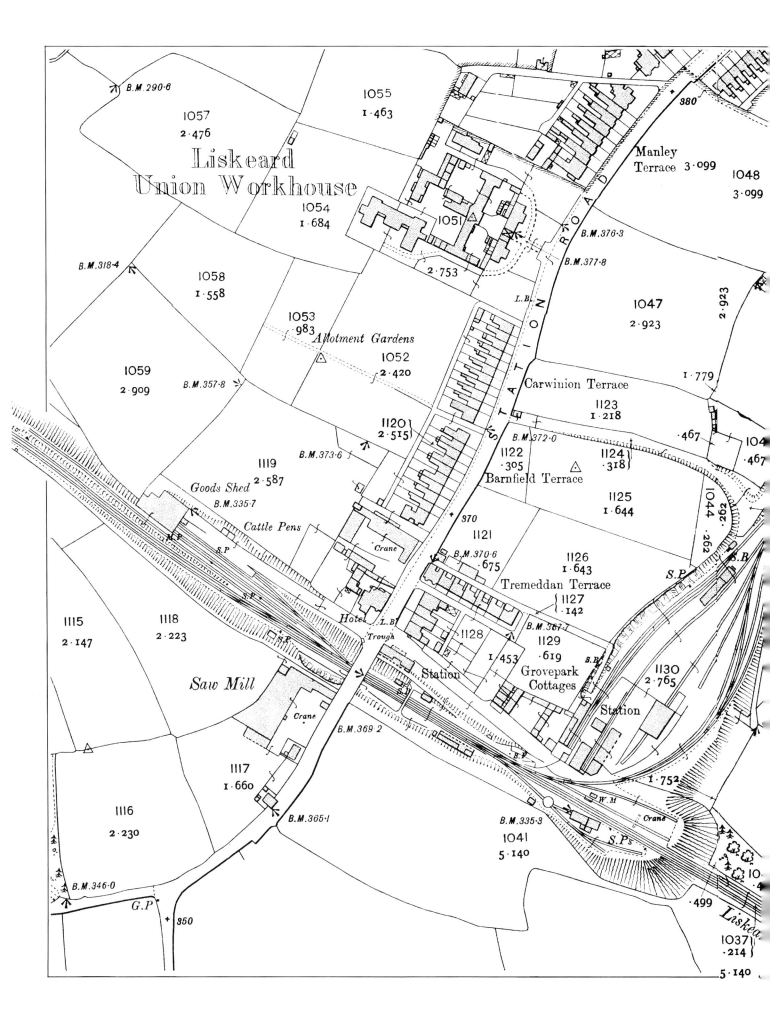

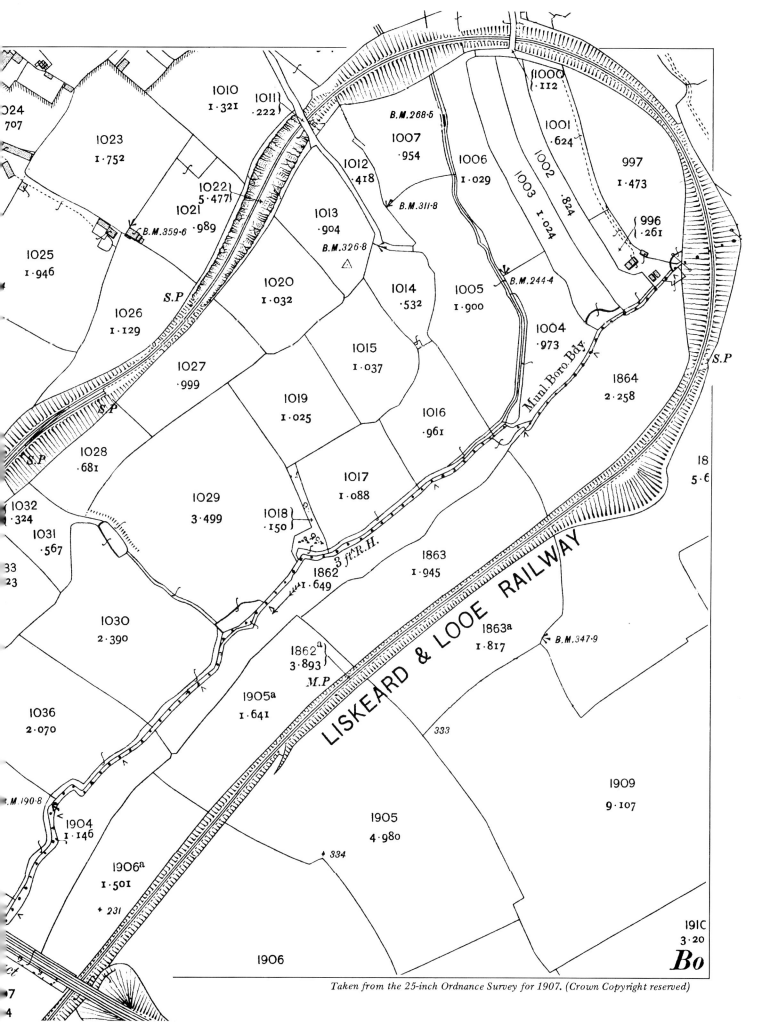

024
·7⁰⁷

1023
1·75²

1010
1·321

1011
·222

1000
·112

B.M.268·5

1007
·954

1001
·624

1006
1·029

1002
·824

1003
1·024

997
1·473

1012
·418

B.M.311·8

1022
5·477

1021
·989

1013
·904

996
·261

B.M.359·6

B.M.326·8

△

1025
1·94⁶

1020
1·032

1014
·532

1005
1·900

B.M.244·4

S.P

1026
1·129

1004
·973

1864
2·258

1027
·999

1015
1·037

Munl. Boro. Bdy.

S.P

S.P

1019
1·025

1016
·961

18
5·6

1028
·681

1032
·324

1029
3·499

1017
1·088

1031
·5⁶⁷

1018
·150

33
23

3 ft. R.H.

1862
1·649

1863
1·945

1030
2·390

1862ᵃ
3·893

1863ᵃ
1·817

B.M.347·9

M.P

1036
2·070

1905ᵃ
1·641

LISKEARD & LOOE RAILWAY

333

1909
9·107

M.190·8

1904
1·14⁶

1905
4·98⁰

·334

1906ᵃ
1·50¹

·231

191C
3·20

·7

4

1906

Bo

ct

Taken from the 25-inch Ordnance Survey for 1907. (Crown Copyright reserved)

Arriving trains usually pulled right up to the buffer stop, then when the passengers had left, the stock was backed along the platform road until clear of the engine release points. After the engine had been uncoupled, it was moved forward again to enable the signalman to reverse the points which released the locomotive to run round its train ready for the next departure. No. 4585 is pictured making this manoeuvre on 29th September 1959.

Peter W. Gray

LISKEARD: LOOE BRANCH STATION

Prior to the construction of the Liskeard and Looe Extension Railway station at Liskeard, the site it later occupied was largely undeveloped. Immediately adjacent to the GWR running line, however, private sidings served the premises of Mr. Charles Isaac, a general merchant. In the broad gauge period a trailing connection from the down line crossed the up line and then ran parallel to it, terminating where the ground fell away and the Liskeard viaduct commenced. Isaac's premises were served by two sidings, which ran off at an acute angle to the GWR siding, access being by means of a wagon turntable. One siding entered Isaac's yard and stores whilst the second went around the edge of the yard to enter a second building which served as a coal store. When the broad gauge was converted to standard gauge, the arrangements remained very similar except that there were then two GWR sidings paralleling the up main line, access to Isaac's siding being from a wagon turntable on the siding closest to his premises.

Construction of the L & LER commenced in 1898 and proved to be a major undertaking for the impecunious local

company. Although the distance from Liskeard to Coombe, where connection with the old line from Looe was to be made, is only three-quarters of a mile as the crow flies, the difference in levels amounted to 205ft. To overcome this difference, the new route climbed to the junction in the form of an elipse, leaving the old line at Coombe in a south-easterly direction. It then turned to face north-east, passing beneath the GWR Liskeard viaduct before turning again through 180 degrees and, climbing all the while, meeting the GWR station from a north-easterly direction. The Liskeard and Looe station was constructed at a right-angle to the GWR main line, to the east of the GWR station and, as already mentioned, connection between the two railways was by means of a sharp curve. Under the terms of the 1895 Act, the line from Coombe to Liskeard was known as Railway No. 1 whilst the connection through the yard to the GWR was known as Railway No. 2.

The length of the new line was 2 miles 5 chains and, due to the heavy engineering works involved, was generally considered to be a major achievement for the small

Passengers leaving a recent arrival from Looe with No. 5531 at the buffer stop.   *Collection R. S. Carpenter*

Ready to depart for Looe. The station building, platform and signal box retained gas lighting until the early 1960s.   *Author's collection*

company. At the completion of the work, the *Cornish Times* reported on the line in detail and related several of the problems that had occurred during construction:

'At Bolitho a landslip occurred during wet weather on the greasy clay bed which had been cut into, and the 5000 cubic yards of stuff which came away had to be tipped on to the big bank under the Liskeard Viaduct, which has thus been made wider than was required, but is correspondingly stronger. Last, but by no means least, a great deal of excavation had to be done to form the station yard at Liskeard — a splendid piece of ground from a railway point of view, which gives the L & L Rly the largest goods yard in Cornwall with the sole exception of the one at Truro. Altogether the amount of cuttings reached about 160,000 cubic yards, exclusive of road diversions and small side cuttings. The total bank filling was, of course, in excess, amounting to as much as 192,000 cubic yards.'

Gradients on the new line were as steep as 1 in 40 and this fact, along with the very sharp curvature involved, imposed limits on the locomotives and rolling stock which could be employed on the line. Indeed these features still restrict the rolling stock available to work the branch to this day — witness the shortlived use of long wheelbase, four-wheeled Class 142 'Pacer' diesel units in 1986.

On the approach to the new Liskeard terminus, the single line emerged from a cutting, then divided, the goods line leading off to the left to make an end-on connection with the exchange sidings, already described, whilst the passenger line continued to terminate beside a platform 195ft long. As well as a pillar tank — for watering locomotives — and a lamp hut, there was a station building which accommodated a booking hall, booking office, parcels office, general waiting room, ladies waiting room and gentlemen's lavatories as well as an open-fronted shelter, all lit by gas. Construction was largely of timber and included a canopy covering the platform to shelter waiting passengers. The station was built close to the premises of Charles Isaac, and due to the construction of the connecting line to the GWR, rail access to his property had to be rearranged so that trucks were henceforth shunted there from the L & LR sidings. Access to the property had extremely tight clearances and special instructions were in force prohibiting covered wagons or open wagons with overhanging loads from Isaac's siding.

Road access to the L & LR station was initially by a cart road from Carwinion Terrace and a footpath which led down to the station from Station Road by way of Tremedden Terrace. Both of these routes were eventually done away with and the GWR station approach road came to serve both stations. Only a very small amount of goods traffic was dealt with at the station, as evidenced by the small goods lock-up provided on the platform adjacent to

Looking south along
the Looe branch plat-
form at Liskeard on
2nd May 1959.
R. M. Casserley

General view along the Looe branch platform showing the signal box and, on the right, the carriage siding added in 1937. The hut on the platform was provided for carriage cleaners whose portable staging for washing coaches can be seen in the yard. The branch coaches were periodically sent to Plymouth Millbay for heavy cleaning.
J. Norris

the buffer stops, the majority of traffic passing to and from the GWR.

Train movements at the terminus were controlled by the L & LR's own signal box. Constructed by Saxby and Farmer, signalling contractors for the 'extension railway', it contained an 18-lever frame and was sited practically opposite the entry to the exchange sidings from where all shunting moves were controlled. The new station was formally opened on 15th May 1901. On the same date the old Liskeard and Looe Railway station at Moorswater was closed, that station having previously served the town, but, in any case, trains from Looe now came only as far as Coombe before reversing direction to face the climb to Liskeard. The new purpose-built station easily coped with

A deserted Looe branch platform in June 1948.   *D. Clayton*

No. 4529 running round its train at Liskeard on 8th May 1948.   *Collection P. Q. Treloar*

A view of the Looe branch yard on 26th May 1956, taken from a train crossing Liskeard viaduct.   *Maurice Dart*

the available traffic and it was not until the L & LR had been fully taken into the GWR fold that any alterations or additions became necessary.

In 1909 the GWR, having taken over responsibility for working the Looe line, applied for the overall speed limit of 10 mph, imposed by the BoT at the opening of the extension line from Liskeard to Coombe, to be raised. Pleading that the limit was a serious hindrance to the working of traffic, and assuring the BoT that the GWR locmotives and rolling stock were well maintained and had sufficient brake power, the authorities at Paddington asked for the limit to be raised to 20 mph. Although the request was conceded to by the BoT, all working instructions give a maximum speed of 15 mph for this section of line.

In 1923 work commenced on extending the passenger platform to 420ft. This work involved removing and refixing the pillar tank to the end of the new platform and at the same time the lamp hut was resited. The newly extended platform was brought into use during April 1924. In 1925 GWR minutes record the voting of funds to rearrange the 'Liskeard and Looe' goods yard at Liskeard but further details have not been found.

During 1936 the platform was again lengthened, to 640ft, being brought into use on 3rd January 1937. Again the pillar tank was resited, and further water works were required in 1937 when two hydrants were installed to serve a new carriage siding which led off the platform engine-release road. These latter works were carried out under the Government's Guaranteed Loans Scheme.

There matters were left for the next twenty years or so and there were few alterations of note until the rationalisation of the branch in the 1960s. With the demise of steam traction and the withdrawal of goods services, the engine release road and a number of sidings were taken out of use and eventually recovered. On 15th March 1964 the Liskeard Branch signal box was closed and subsequently demolished. In more recent years, much of the yard area has been given over to car parking and since 1986 a

park-and-ride scheme has been in operation in an attempt to overcome the appalling road traffic congestion in the streets of Looe. The original Liskeard and Looe Railway station building, however, remains intact at present as a memorial to the ambitions of the independent railway.

On leaving the platform, trains departing Liskeard for Looe first passed the signal box on the left and crossed a small accommodation bridge before the goods line joined the main running line from the right. In the GWR period, departing trains were controlled by a starting signal, sited at the foot of the platform ramp, and an advanced starting signal sited clear of the yard points near the mouth of the cutting. Goods trains, or empty passenger stock, leaving the sidings and passing on to the branch proper, were controlled by a shunting signal with a ringed arm in the GWR style.

A shallow reverse curve took the line across an embankment before it entered a cutting and commenced a descent at 1 in 60, steepening to 1 in 40. Two overbridges carried lanes over the line as a curve of about 8 chains radius took the line through 180 degrees around the head of the valley and past the Liskeard fixed distant. This signal had an unusual lamp casing with a lens in the side, as well as the lens facing forward towards approaching trains, which enabled the signalman in the Liskeard Branch signal box, almost opposite but way across the valley, to check that the lamp was alight during the hours of darkness. The descent continued – for some distance still at 1 in 80 – and took the line beneath the GWR Liskeard viaduct. To the left of the continuously braking train, in due course, the GWR Bolitho viaduct could be seen, on the main line towards Menheniot and Plymouth, whilst the branch again curves sharply to the right through 90 degrees. Still descending steeply, the line enters a deep cutting, spanned by Lodge Hill bridge. The gradient at this point was still falling, at 1 in 38, and an embankment then took the line over a road and towards the junction with the line from Looe at Coombe.

This view was taken on 7th August 1961 and shows No. 4574 in the distance about to collect the 'B set' from No. 5553 which had recently arrived from Looe. The coaches were then added to No. 4574's own train of three coaches, already standing at the platform and packed to capacity. Such was the demand for Looe on this August Bank Holiday.

P. Barnfield

One of the two branch 'B sets' and one of the specially allocated strengthening vehicles, standing on the carriage siding at Liskeard in June 1948.

D. Clayton

Looe branch water tank at Liskeard in August 1963.

P. J. Garland

No. 4552 arriving at Liskeard with empty coaching stock on 17th July 1960 with the signalman leaning from the window of his 'box to collect the single line tablet from the fireman.

R. C. Riley

An up train arriving at Liskeard in September 1961. Having reached the summit of the climb from Coombe Junction, drivers had usually eased off by this point before entering the station. *G. Tilt*

The Looe branch home signals and the headshunt of the goods yard at Liskeard in August 1963.
P. J. Garland

Looking down the 1 in 55 gradient towards Coombe Junction in August 1963.   *P. J. Garland*

A closer view of the prohibition notice visible in the view above.
                                                            P. J. Garland

An up train nearing the summit, with the engine still working hard on the climb to Liskeard in June 1948.   *D. Clayton*

This farm accommodation overbridge was the first from Liskeard, its tall stone abutments and 15ft span semi-circular brick arch carrying a 12ft 6in roadway over the line 8 miles 39½ chains from Looe.

P. J. Garland

The second stone-built overbridge, 8 miles 31½ chains from Looe, carried another 12ft 6in farm lane, this time by means of a segmental brick arch with a 15ft span.

P. J. Garland

The Liskeard fixed distant signal
with the lamp specially adapted
so that the back light was visible
to the signalman across the valley.
Photographed in August 1963.

P. J. Garland

No. 4552 making the climb from Coombe Junction with empty coaching stock on 17th July 1960.   *R. C. Riley*

An up train headed by No. 5539 near the Liskeard viaduct on 19th June 1959.   *R. J. Sellick*

When the Liskeard and Looe Extension Railway was built beneath the Liskeard viaduct, it was required to pay the GWR an easement fee of £3 per annum for the privilege although the GWR paid only £1 per annum for the similar facility of crossing the L & CR line by the Moorswater viaduct! This view along the Looe branch shows the reconstructed Liskeard viaduct on 9th November 1926.

National Railway Museum

No. 4574 on the 4.35 p.m. Liskeard to Looe train cautiously descending to Coombe Junction on 6th August 1961. The bridge in the background is the Bolitho viaduct, on the main line east of Liskeard.

Peter W. Gray

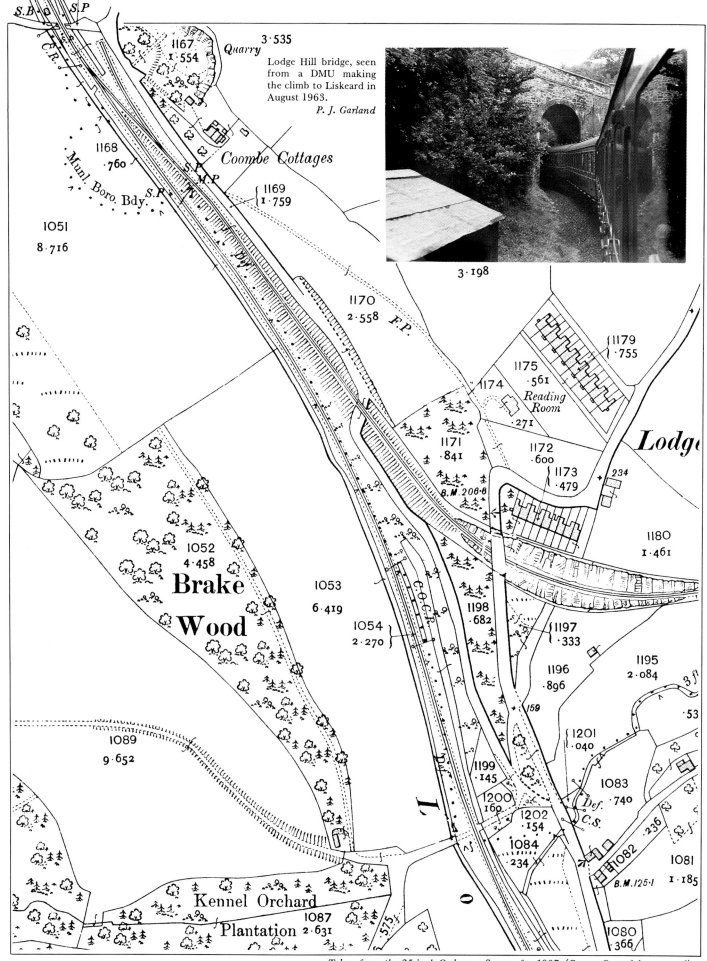

S.B. S.P

C.R.

3·535

1167
1·554

Quarry

Lodge Hill bridge, seen
from a DMU making
the climb to Liskeard in
August 1963.

P. J. Garland

1168
·760

S·M·P

Coombe Cottages

Munl Boro. Bdy.

S.P

1169
1·759

1051
8·716

1170
2·558

F.P.

3·198

1179
·755

1175
·561

1174

Reading
Room
·271

Lodge

1171
·841

1172
·600

1173
·479

234

B.M. 206·6

1052
4·458

1180
1·461

Brake

1053

Wood

6·419

1198
·682

1197
·333

1195
2·084

3 ft

C.O.C.R.

1196
·896

·53

1054
2·270

159

1201
·040

1083
·740

Def.
C.S.

·236

1089
9·652

Duf

1199
·145

1200
·160

1202
·154

1082

1081
1·185

1084
·234

B.M. 125·1

575

Kennel Orchard

1080
·366

Plantation 2·631

1087

Taken from the 25-inch Ordnance Survey for 1907. (Crown Copyright reserved)

COOMBE JUNCTION

The remarkable arrangements at Coombe Junction are one of the more distinctive features of the Liskeard and Looe branch, underlining the line's individuality. Its attractive setting in the East Looe river valley made the station a starting point for walkers and a haunt for generations of railway enthusiasts with an eye for the picturesque and unusual.

At first there was no stopping place at Coombe on the line from Looe to Moorswater. A passenger station, adjacent to the GWR viaduct, was provided at Moorswater to serve the town of Liskeard and only the narrow road to Coombe House crossed the line on the level at Coombe by an occupation crossing. Around 250 yards north of the level crossing, a stone overbridge carried a minor road from Liskeard across the line, the nearby hamlet of Lamellion lending its name to the bridge which was numbered seventh from Looe. Bridges were numbered from Looe to Liskeard and the line also was measured from Looe, originally to Caradon and later to the terminus at Liskeard. This practice dates from the independent company and was opposite to

the usual GWR system where mileage was measured from the junction to the terminus. Mileage was marked on mile stones at first, and some of them remained in position until well into GWR ownership.

In 1884 it was suggested that an additional stopping place should be provided at Coombe for the benefit of passengers going to the GWR station at Liskeard. Although only three-quarters of a mile separated the two stations, the road from Coombe was steeply graded but was no doubt more convenient than reaching the GWR station from Moorswater along a road which passed through the town of Liskeard. The Coombe station was probably brought into use immediately and was certainly in use by 1896 when trains could be stopped for passengers to alight on giving prior notice to the guard.

By 1898 when the Liskeard and Looe Extension Railway was under construction, it was proposed to provide a station where the new line made its junction with the old. A loop measuring 650ft overall was provided, with a cross-over about halfway along its length. Originally the platform

This view shows No. 5531 climbing from Coombe Junction on 20th August 1961 and about to pass beneath Lodge Hill bridge.

M. J. Messenger

was built of old sleepers and, measuring only 90ft in length, was erected close to the adjacent Duchy Tweed Mills. By 1923, however, when the GWR had absorbed the line, the platform had been reconstructed with a stone facing, and provided with a wooden shelter and oil lamps. Coombe Junction opened to traffic on 15th May 1901, along with the connecting line to Liskeard, and the old station at Moorswater closed on the same day.

Train movements at the new junction were controlled from a signal box equipped with a catch handle locking frame with 26 levers (20 working and 6 spare) and a gate wheel for the level crossing. Supplied by Saxby and Farmer, the 'box was of timber construction, with a slate roof, and was identical to that provided at Liskeard at the same time. New crossing gates were also provided. The original occupation gates, which were normally left closed to road traffic and opened away from the track, remained in situ. Interestingly, the BoT inspecting officer commented that the station was rather over-elaborately signalled given the amount of traffic.

Trains running between Looe and Liskeard entered the platform and remained there while the engine ran from one end of the train to the other for the reversal. The points releasing the engine from the headshunt onto the loop were spring-loaded latterly although photographs suggest that earlier they were worked by hand lever. Strict rules applied to this operation and locomotives were prohibited from being detached from a train at the platform if another train was standing on the adjacent line as, of course, there was no means of locking the engine release road to protect the train standing on the loop.

Trains approaching Coombe Junction descended cautiously down the 1 in 40 gradient from Liskeard at the regulation 15 mph until they reached the home signal about 100 yds from the junction. If the signal remained at 'danger', the driver would give a 'crow' on the engine whistle to warn the Coombe Junction signalman of the train's presence. If the train was brought to a stand at the home signal, a system of whistle codes was used to enable the train driver to advise the signalman of the route required into the station. The full code is appended overleaf and a similar but simplified code was employed through the GWR and BR(W) periods until the service was rationalized upon the introduction of diesel power.

Beyond the signal, a runaway siding protected the junction and the station from out-of-control trains. The further end of this siding received little, if any, maintenance and retained the original bullhead rail resting in L&LR chairs until well into the 1970s when it was examined by the writer. It is recorded that, from time to time, possibly between 1910 and 1920, this siding was used for unloading coal traffic, which perhaps rather detracts from the sidings' function as an emergency run-off siding.

In 1906, when the set of coaches ran away down the gradient from Liskeard, the signalman was advised of the out-of-control train by telephone and very promptly set the road for the coaches to run straight through the station and on to Moorswater, presumably hoping that they would

lose momentum and eventually come to rest. Signalman Edmund Marsh also stopped the up train from Looe, which was approaching the junction and undoubtedly saved the lives of a group of children who were playing in the road at the end of the run-off siding. Signalman Marsh received due commendation. His salary is recorded elsewhere as 21 shillings per week, which compared favourably with GWR signalmen of similar grade at this period. Following the takeover by the GWR, the former Liskeard and Looe employees very soon moved on, being transferred away from the area. In 1909 signalmen Marsh and Husband were employed at Coombe Junction, but in due course they transferred away, Marsh going to Wrangaton on the South Devon main line. Their places were taken by Rufus Parsons, a GWR man from Perranporth, and on the opposite shift by Thomas Dodd, another GWR man who came from Goonbarrow Junction. Other than the signalmen, the station was unstaffed, coming under the jurisdiction of the Liskeard station master.

Trains arriving at Coombe Junction, from either Liskeard or Looe, were limited to a speed of 10 mph when negotiating the junction and passenger trains would enter the platform by either of the crossovers.

Full instructions on the operation of both passenger and goods trains were issued by Holbrook, the L&LR traffic manager and are reproduced herewith to illustrate the working of this most unusual station:

Coombe Junction

A platform has been erected at Coombe Junction for the accommodation of Passengers, and the Engines of all trains travelling from Looe to Liskeard or vice versa, must run round their trains, after bringing the vehicles to a stand at this platform. A pair of points (self-acting) are provided at the Bridge End of the Platform Road to enable them to do so, these points will fall back into proper position after the Engine has passed through them, and enginemen must see that they do this.

Two crossover roads called respectively A & B give access to this Platform Road. Crossover B is the crossover nearest the Coombe Junct. Signal Cabin; both these crossovers are worked by the signalman from that Box; crossover A being provided with a 'ground disc' signal, i.e. for the purpose of allowing Engine Drivers to back on to the other end of their train for the outward journey and no driver must go back on to the train until this 'ground disc' signal is turned.

As the platform road leads to a 'dead end', drivers must have their trains well under control before entering it, prepared to stop at the Platform. Guards must also keep a good look out and apply 'Hand Brakes' if necessary to ensure this; and great care must be exercised by all concerned.

A run-away road is also provided on the main line as shewn above, *, leading to a dead end, and the points leading to it will lay normally for the dead end, except when required otherwise, for the passage of Engines and trains; this runaway road is intended to protect trains passing through crossings A and B, from any vehicle or traffic coming from Moorswater in the direction of the Coombe Cabin.

The usual mode of working will be as follows; all ordinary 'PASSENGER' trains will enter and leave the platform by way of crossover A; but if these passenger trains are at any time made up to more vehicles than can be admitted to the platform via crossover A at Coombe Jct, the Liskeard or the Looe signalman respectively will be held responsible for advising the 'Coombe Jct' signalman of this, so that the train may be admitted via

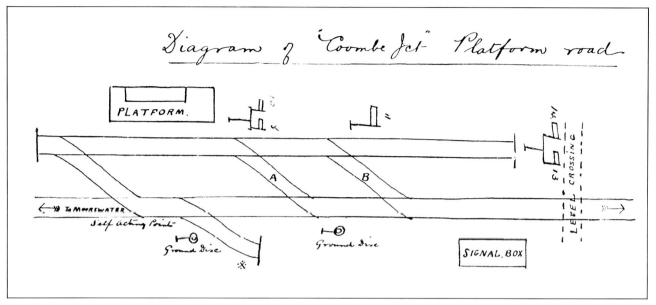

crossover B instead; and Drivers and Guards must be prepared to act accordingly.

All GOODS trains requiring to enter this platform road for the purpose of Engines running round, will both enter and leave by way of crossing B.

If two trains both for the platform road arrive at the Junction Home Signals, at the same time, the one first to be admitted to the platform will be allowed to enter this platform road by way of crossover A or B as required; after the Engine has run round its train and the work at the platform is completed, No. 10 (i.e. the left-hand signal on the two arm post at the end of the platform) will be lowered for the driver to draw on to signal No. 11, and there he must wait until that signal is lowered, which will be after the second train has passed to the platform via crossover A. The train then waiting at signal No. 11 will be allowed to proceed on its journey by way of crossover B, before the Engine of the second train is allowed to run round its train. The Driver and Guard of the first train, which has been allowed to draw on to signal No. 11, will be held responsible for seeing that the 'Tail End' of their train stands clear of the points of crossover A, and if necessary to do this, must draw down steadily to the dead end for that purpose; but not until first having stopped at No. 11 signal, and the driver must advise the signalman of what they are doing by means of 4 short sharp whistles.

Except for this purpose, no driver must allow his train or Engine to stand upon the 'Locking Bars' which extend about 3 yards beyond the tongue of certain points.

If the second train to be admitted to the Platform is too long to admit or is going to the platform via crossover A, it must run quite beyond the train waiting on the platform road, and then after the first train has left, and upon being called back by the signalman (by use of a green flag by day and green light by night) back steadily, until it can enter the platform via crossover B.

A code of engine whistles, as per following clauses, will be in force and when approaching the Junction the Engine Driver must give the required notice by whistle if the signals are at Danger, if the proper signals however are lowered for him to proceed, he must not give the Junction Whistles.

If on approaching a Junction the Driver finds a wrong signal has been lowered for him, he must bring his train to a stand and sound the proper Junction Whistle, so as to give the signalman an opportunity of altering the points and lowering the signal for the proper line. Should, however, the wrong signal still remain off, the FIREMAN in the case of a Light Engine, or of a train with only one Guard or with two Guards both riding in the rear, and the FRONT GUARD in the case of a train with two Guards, one riding in front, must at once proceed to the Signal Box and inform the Signalman what train it is, in order that the Signalman may alter the Points and Signals, or give authority for the train to pass along the Line for which the Signal was first lowered.

For trains approaching 'Coombe Jct' from Looe or Liskeard, a three armed bracket 'Signal Post' is provided to protect the level crossing gates to Coombe, as follows.

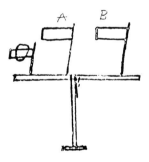

The short one on the extreme left is for trains to Moorswater.

The middle Signal for trains to the platform via crossover A.

The Signal on the extreme right for trains to the Platform via crossover B.

Drivers must approach the Home Signals with great care, prepared to stop at these Signals, even though the Distant Signals may have been off.

A runaway road is placed just inside the Home Signal of the New Line from Liskeard at Coombe, viz on the Signal Box side of the Signal post; this road will always lay for the Dead End so long as that Home Signal remains at Danger, thus protecting traffic passing on the Looe Line.

Trains leaving the platform road for the New Line must first have Signals No. 10, 11 & 14 lowered before proceeding on the journey.

A down train easing into Coombe Junction on 11th August 1951.   *H. F. Wheeller*

No. 4561 approaching Coombe Junction with a train from Liskeard on 18th August 1959.   *P. Hay*

A Signal is also provided, viz on the 'Overline Bridge' at Coombe, and no train or Engine, passing from the direction of Moorswater, must pass this Signal when at danger.

All exchange of TABLETS will be made as the Drivers pass the Coombe Signal Box, and proper pouches holding the tablets (which are visible) will be provided for this purpose.

Drivers must, before proceeding, see that the correct tablet for the Section they require to run in, has been handed them.

ENGINE WHISTLES

Liskeard Line. Home Signal to Junction Bracket Signals	1 long	
Looe Line	Home Signal to Junction Bracket Signal	1 long, 1 short
Bracket Junction Signal (3 arms) to Moorswater	1 short	
Bracket Junction Signal (3 arm post) to platform via Crossover B	2 short	
Bracket Junction Signal (3 arm post) to platform via Crossover A	3 short	
Out of Platform to Main Line via Crossover A for Liskeard	1 short, 1 long	
Out of Platform to Main Line via Crossover A for Looe Line	2 short, 1 long	
Out of Platform to Main Line via Crossover B (or to Signal No. 11) for Liskeard	3 short, 1 long	
Out of Platform to Main Line via Crossover B (or to Signal No. 11) for Looe Line	3 short given twice	
Home Signal on Bridge Moorswater to Coombe	2 long	
To draw past No. 11 Signal to Dead End for clearing A points, as previous explained.	4 sharp short whistles	

Following the takeover by the GWR, some of the Saxby & Farmer signals were fitted with replacement GWR arms and lamps, whilst in due course replacement signals of standard GWR design appeared. The goods 'home' signal, giving access to Coombe Junction from Moorswater, was mounted on a concrete post of the pattern used by the GWR around the grouping in 1923. This signal was of necessity mounted on a tall post to enable it to be seen above Lamellion Bridge by the Coombe Junction signalman.

By December 1928 the middle crossover had been removed and the signalling was amended at the same time. Curiously, the platform was never lengthened, which perhaps reflects the small amount of traffic which originated or terminated at the station. With the introduction of the motor economic system of maintenance to the line in 1931, a run-off was constructed, leading from the goods line, and a sleeper-built shed accommodated the motor trolley and its trailer. The gang responsible for permanent way maintenance of the branch was based at Coombe Junction. A corrugated lamp hut was sited near to the signal box — but not too close, for safety reasons — whilst a setting-down post was provided for the single-line train tablet, although in practice it was seldom used as exchanges took place with the signalman at the signal box window.

Thus matters remained until February 1956 when the life-expired Saxby & Farmer lever frame was replaced by a GWR 5-bar vertical tappet lever frame containing 26 levers. At the same time a bracket signal replaced the Coombe

Running round at Coombe Junction on 7th August 1961.
P. Barnfield

A detail view of the level crossing gates at Coombe Junction which had been replaced in 1956.   *D. J. Hyde*

Junction to Looe or Liskeard starting signals, whilst a disc signal replaced the goods line starting signals. At an earlier date the old three-arm bracket signal controlling access to the goods line or platform road, had been replaced, and all these new signals were constructed in the contemporary GWR postwar steel-gantry style on tubular steel posts with enamelled steel arms. The original Saxby & Farmer level crossing gates also remained in use until this time and were replaced with substantial new timber gates.

Coombe Junction level crossing gates and the bracketed home signals controlling access to the platform or goods lines in August 1978.
M. J. Mitchell

Another view from Coombe Junction signal box, this time showing No. 4552 arriving with a down train on 4th July 1959.
Peter W. Gray

Rear view of Coombe Junction signal box in August 1978.
M. J. Mitchell

A feature of operation in the latter days of steam was the daily crossing of passenger trains at Coombe Junction. Larry Crozier, a relief signalman in the Plymouth area in the 1950s, worked Coombe Junction signal box on occasions, providing relief for the regular men, Dick Hoare and Cyril Shapley. He has provided an account of the movements required to cross passenger trains, which reads thus:

'The signalman would receive "Train out of Section" from Looe at roughly 9.25 a.m. for the 8.55 Liskeard passenger. When the signal was acknowledged, Looe would ask "Is Line Clear" for the 9.45 up passenger which would be accepted under Regulation 5 (The Warning Arrangement). The next move would be about 9.33 when two blasts on an engine whistle heralded the 9.30 light engine from Moorswater shed approaching the Home signal (this line was classed as a siding). After receiving Line Clear from Liskeard Branch Box, the signals would be lowered and the engine would proceed after taking the token, this could conveniently be handed out of the window. The signals would be restored to Danger and peace would reign supreme, broken only by the "Train out of Section" signal from Liskeard. The long awaited "Train Entering Section" signal would be received from Looe at 9.45 denoting the train was away on time.

'The fun would start when the Liskeard Branch signalman asked clear for the 9.55 passenger as it was starting from that station. The road would be set for the platform line and the signals lowered. As soon as the train stopped at Coombe Jcn. platform, the engine was uncoupled and proceeded clear of the spring points. The engine would then return through the Goods line, and return to the other end of its train. The same promptness was shown in recoupling and the train would pull out past the box, then set back on the Goods. By this time the 9.45 ex Looe had arrived at the Home signal and would be admitted to the platform line. After the necessary bell signals had been exchanged and the token withdrawn, the 9.55 ex Liskeard would leave the Goods line leaving it clear for the other engine to run around its train. Again prompt action by the train crew would see the train off to Liskeard. The time taken between the first train arriving at the platform till the second left for Liskeard never exceeded five minutes.'

Following the end of steam in 1961, the engine release crossover was removed in June 1963. The signal box remained in use for almost another two decades, becoming increasingly an anachronism as an oasis of mechanical signalling on an otherwise rationalized and modernised railway system. Closure eventually came on 8th May 1981, when the signal box was taken out of use. It is probable that if the box had not closed, it would have fallen down within a short time, as when the writer visited the location shortly before its demise, the structure was in an advanced state of decay. Movements at Coombe Junction were subsequently controlled from a ground frame operated by the guard, the diesel multiple units employed on the line having to stop at the approach to the junction to set down the guard for this purpose.

Once the driver had received the 'right away' from the guard, trains leaving Coombe Junction for Looe proceeded steadily to the signal box, where the signalman would hand the token from the signal box window. Once over the level crossing and after negotiating the junction at the regulation 10 mph, trains accelerated away down the 1 in 121 gradient towards Looe.

With the 'extension' line to Liskeard climbing steeply and curving away to the east, the road from Liskeard, having descended Lodge Hill, joined the railway to run side by side down the valley. About a third of a mile from the junction of the two railway routes, a side road leading to Lodge Barton crossed the line on the level, the gates here being closed across the road and opening away from the line.

Shortly afterwards, the Coombe Junction Distant signal was passed; this was a standard GWR fixed caution board, latterly on a tubular steel post, which remained in situ until the 1980s.

Coombe Junction signal box with Coombe House visible in the background.

D. J. Hyde

Detail of the coal bunker and signalmen's privy at Coombe Junction.

D. J. Hyde

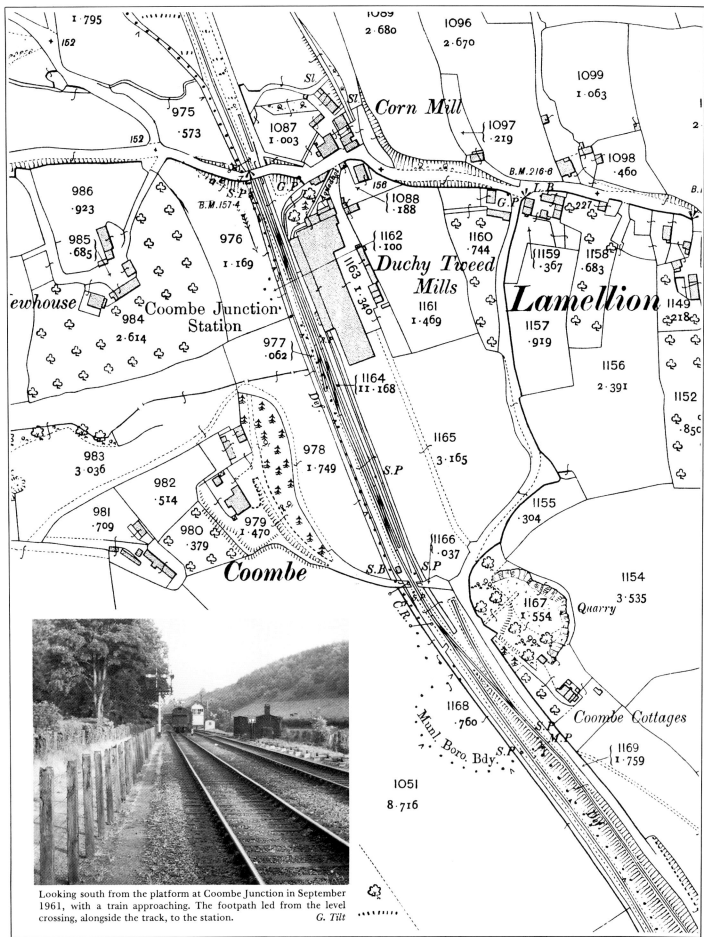

I · 795

· 152

1089
2 · 680

1096
2 · 670

975
· 573

152

1087
I · 003

Sl

Sl

Corn Mill

1097
· 219

1099
I · 063

1098
· 460

B.M. 216·6

986
· 923

S.P
B.M. 157·4

G.P

156

1088
· 188

L.B

G.P

227

985
· 685

976
I · 169

1162
· 100

1160
· 744

1159
· 367

1158
· 683

ewhouse

984
2 · 614

*Coombe Junction
Station*

1163 I · 340

*Duchy Tweed
Mills*

1161
I · 469

Lamellion

1157
· 919

1149
· 218

977
· 062

1164
11 · 168

1156
2 · 391

1152
· 850

983
3 · 036

978
I · 749

982
· 514

981
· 709

979
I · 470

980
· 379

Coombe

S.P

1165
3 · 165

1155
· 304

1166
· 037

S.P

S.B.

1154
3 · 535

1167
I · 554

Quarry

C.R.

Coombe Cottages

1168
· 760

Munl. Boro. Bdy.

S.P

M.P

S.P

1169
I · 759

1051
8 · 716

Looking south from the platform at Coombe Junction in September
1961, with a train approaching. The footpath led from the level
crossing, alongside the track, to the station.   *G. Tilt*

Taken from the 25-inch Ordnance Survey for 1907. (Crown Copyright reserved)

Coombe Junction station, looking north in 1952.   *P. J. Garland*

The view from Coombe Junction station towards Moorswater, with Lamellion bridge immediately beyond the headshunt and Moorswater viaduct in the distance.

Hugh Davies

Looking south from Lamellion bridge on 13th June 1957.

R. J. Sellick

A misty day at Coombe Junction with the engine running round and disinterested children.   *J. Norris*

No. 4552 running round in 1952. The engine release point was sprung-loaded, thus saving the fireman from having to climb down from the engine. In earlier years the point was worked by a weighted hand lever (see page 56).   *P. J. Garland*

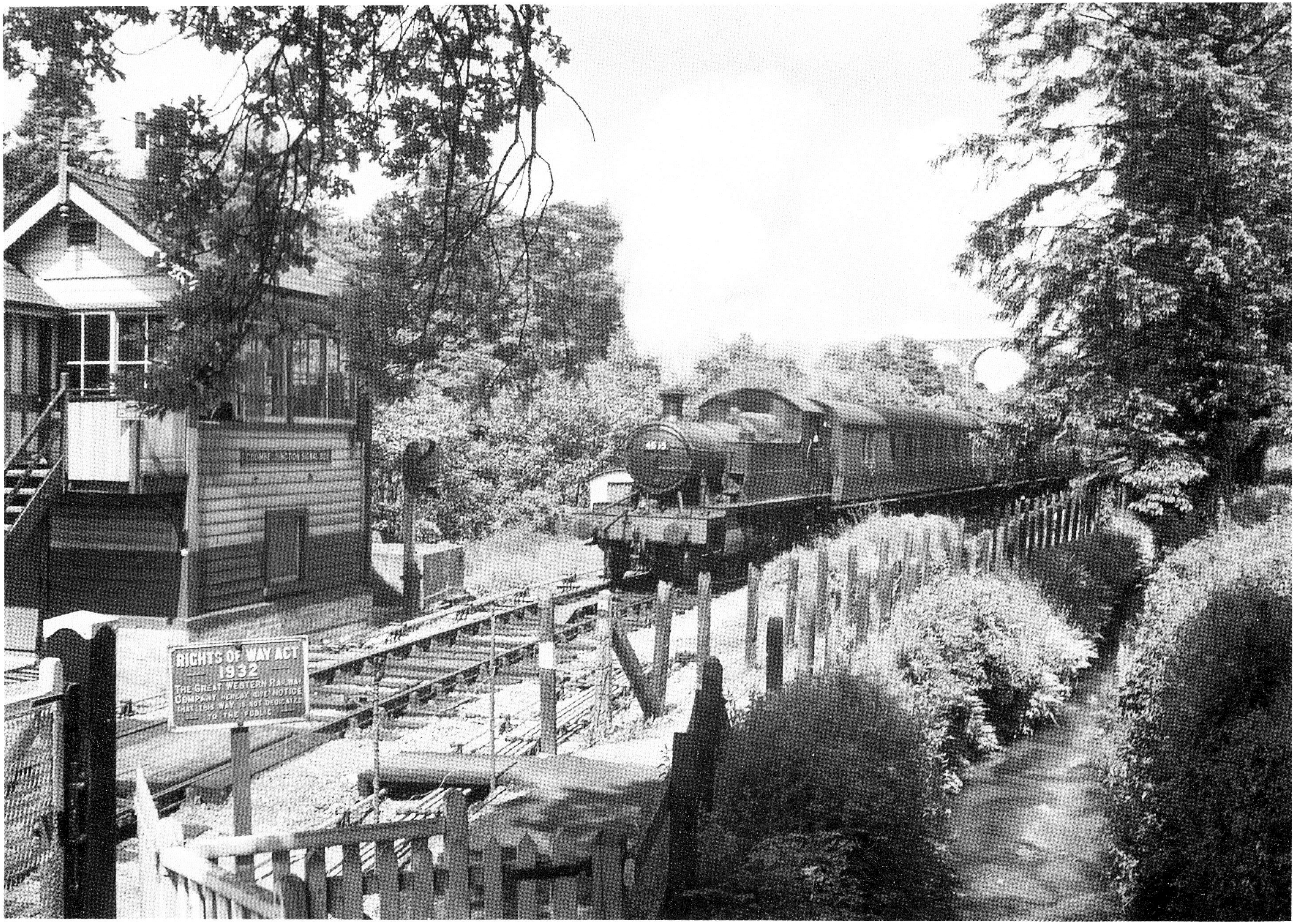
COOMBE JUNCTION SIGNAL BOX
4535
RIGHTS OF WAY ACT
1932
THE GREAT WESTERN RAILWAY
COMPANY HEREBY GIVE NOTICE
THAT THIS WAY IS NOT DEDICATED
TO THE PUBLIC

No. 4535 departing from Coombe Junction in the 1950s.

Collection R. S. Carpenter

A view from the signal box of No. 4574 leaving Coombe Junction for Looe in September 1961.

G. Tilt

No. 4559 heading for Looe with the 5.55 p.m. from Liskeard on 7th May 1960.

Peter W. Gray

No. 4552 with a down train approaching Lodge level crossing on 17th July 1960.   *R. C. Riley*

A latterday view of Lodge level crossing.
D. J. Hyde

ST. KEYNE

Once the railway from Coombe Junction has left the vicinity of the earthworks bringing the line from Liskeard, the course of the old canal becomes apparent alongside. The earthworks of the new line obliterated the canal, and for passengers travelling to Looe, the former waterway becomes apparent for the first time in the vicinity of Trussell Bridge. Here an overbridge carries a lane across the railway before it curves due south to run to St. Keyne. As with Coombe, there was no stopping place at St. Keyne for many years. A road crosses the line by an overbridge at this point and adjacent to the railway stood the St. Keyne Roller Flour Mills for which, in 1886, it was proposed to provide a siding. This came to nothing but by the turn of the century there were moves afoot to construct a station. Petitions to the railway company were received from the inhabitants of the parishes of Duloe and St. Keyne and the southern districts of Liskeard requesting the provision of a stopping place at St. Keyne and by 1902 the proposal was under consideration. The tender of J. Alderman of West Looe was accepted for the construction of the platform, with a front wall of masonry measuring 200ft in length and

3ft in height. The shelter was constructed from secondhand materials lying at Moorswater. The new station appeared in the public timetable for the first time in October 1902.

Although a contemporary article described the waiting shelter as being of wooden construction with 'a nameboard over its doorway', all photographs show the shelter to be clad in corrugated iron sheeting. Access to the station was by a path leading down from the adjacent road, near the overbridge, and entry to the platform was by means of a gate next to the shelter. The only other items on the platform were a wooden bench seat and an oil lamp. Alongside the platform, at the Looe end, were the remains of a lime kiln, whilst the course of the former canal was visible opposite the platform.

As well as local traffic, the station very soon attracted a healthy patronage from visitors who arrived by train to view the famous tree-covered St. Keyne's well. Sited just over half a mile from the station, the well is something of a mystery and was restored by the Old Cornwall Society in 1936. Legend has it that St. Keyne travelled throughout the land in the 6th century before settling in Cornwall. She

A down train in the charge of No. 4565 arriving at St. Keyne on 13th June 1957.

R. J. Sellick

No. 4569 with the 4.35 p.m. train from Liskeard arriving at St. Keyne on 9th August 1960.   *H. B. Priestley*

apparently blessed the waters of this well so that when a couple came to drink, the first to sip the waters would gain mastery throughout the marriage. It was a well established custom by the Victorian era for newlyweds to race each other to the well and it was a popular attraction even before St. Keyne station was opened. Indeed, such was the importance of the well as a source of traffic, that the nameboard over the doorway of the platform shelter advised passengers to alight 'For St. Keyne Well'.

Despite its appearance, it was never known as a halt, and throughout its existence St. Keyne has been unstaffed. During the Great Western period, it came under the supervision of the Looe station master, who was required to visit the station from time to time to check the premises and ensure that the gates, notice boards, shelter, seats, etc, were in order.

Station nameboard in 1966.
C. L. Caddy

St. Keyne, looking towards Coombe Junction on 5th July 1952. Surviving records show that when the station was built in 1902 it had a masonry platform wall, but this view clearly shows a timber structure.
G. A. Hookham

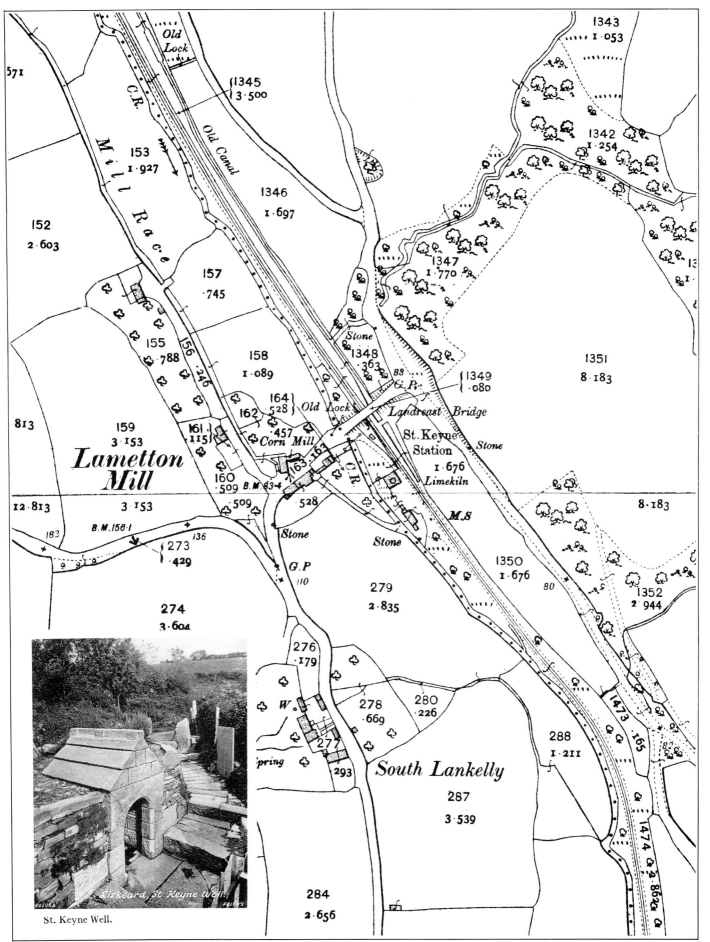

Old
Lock

C.R.

1345
3·500

571

153
1·927

152
2·603

Mill Race

1346
1·697

157
·745

1343
1·053

1342
1·254

155
·788

156
·246

158
1·089

813

164
·528

Old Lock

162

Corn Mill

·457

159
3·153

161
·115

160
·509

B.M. 83·4

Lametton
Mill

Stone

1348
·363

1347
1·770

1351
8·183

88
G.P.

1349
·080

Landreast Bridge

St. Keyne
Station
1·676

Stone

163
·162

C.R.

Limekiln

12·813

3·153

183

B.M. 156·1

136

273
·429

509

528

G.P
·110

Stone

Stone

M.S

8·183

1350
1·676

80

1352
2·944

274
3·604

276
·179

279
2·835

W.

278
·669

280
·226

288
1·211

1473
·165

pring

277

South Lankelly

293

287
3·539

1474
2·862a

284
2·656

St. Keyne Well.

No. 4574 with a down train in September 1961.

G. Tilt

An up train consisting of two 'B sets' arriving at St. Keyne. When compared with the view on page 58 it will be seen that the lime kiln had disappeared.

S. J. Dickson

Surprisingly, there is a suggestion in official records of possible closure in 1907, along with the other wayside stations at Causeland and Sandplace. However, this did not happen and the station duly passed into GWR ownership. In 1910 the overbridge carrying the road over the line was reconstructed to improve clearances and allow the use of GWR carriage stock. Since then there have been few alterations to speak of, and the station remains to this day practically unchanged since it was opened in 1902.

Just below St. Keyne station the old canal goes under the line by a culvert, whilst the road which had run alongside the railway, almost from Coombe Junction, left the valley and climbed to the hamlet at Trewidland. The railway in this vicinity was still laid on granite blocks in 1901 and the fragile permanent way required constant attention and rapid replacement. As the railway approached Landlooe Bridge, about a mile from St. Keyne station, the valley began to narrow, and here the railway was built on the course of the former canal.

The road came down into the valley from Trewidland to rejoin the railway and crossed the line by a bridge. Further down the valley, the former canal was again to be seen on the west of the line, although usually covered in dense undergrowth.

Landlooe bridge, south of St. Keyne station, is exactly four miles from Looe. This view was taken on 7th July 1986. *Author*

View from a down train between St. Keyne and Causeland. *Collection R. S. Carpenter*

The romantically situated Causeland station in September 1961.

G. Tilt

CAUSELAND

Below Landlooe Bridge the valley becomes more intimate, with the valley sides rising steeply away from the line, and the road — little more than a lane, really — following the railway and the river along the valley floor. It is in the area of Causeland station that the oft-repeated description of the line — 'like travelling along a country lane' — particularly applies, as the luxuriant vegetation seems to close in upon the train. Indeed, an account of a journey along the line appeared in the *Railway Magazine* in its issue of March 1899 which conveys such an impression. An extract reads:

> 'The course of the railway is along the bed of a disused canal, and from the train the scenery is magnificent, although the pleasure of the ride is somewhat marred by the incessant jolting. We proceeded along a deep valley, the sides of which were covered with trees, occasionally by open spaces, where we saw whitewashed cottages and disused mines; under three or four bridges, the sides of which came uncomfortably close to the carriage windows, while in other places the boughs of the trees almost seemed to brush the sides of our train. At length a terrific screech from 'Kilmar' warned us that we were approaching a station, and very soon we pulled up at Causeland Station, which consists of merely a platform on which is erected a sleeper hut — like a platelayer's — but without even a door, over the entrance to which is placed a board with the name of the station in black letters on a white ground. Not a cottage is

Guard Stan Salter attending to a passenger at Causeland on 11th August 1951. As well as his railway duties, Stan had civic responsibilities and was later a Mayor of Liskeard. *H. F. Wheeler*

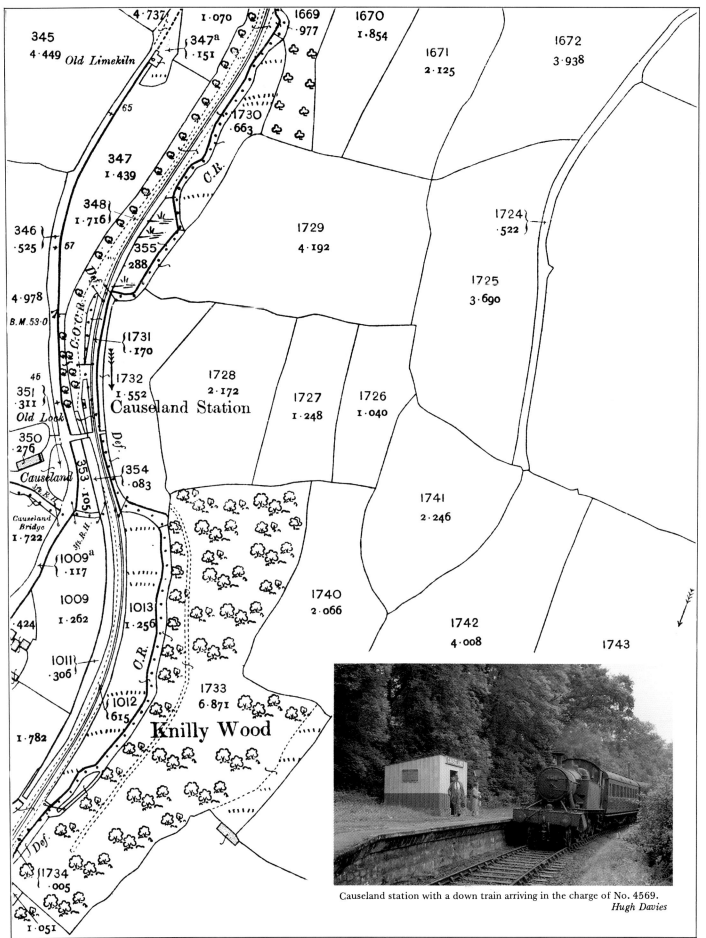

345
4·449 *Old Limekiln*

4·737

1·070

1669
·977

1670
1·854

1671
2·125

1672
3·938

347ª
·151

65

1730
·663

C.R.

347
1·439

1729
4·192

1724
·522

348
1·716

1725
3·690

346
·525

67

355
288

4·978

B.M.53·0

1731
·170

45

1732
1·552

Causeland Station

1728
2·172

1727
1·248

1726
1·040

351
·311
Old Lock

350
·276

353
·105

354
·083

1741
2·246

Causeland

Causeland Bridge
1·722

1009ª
·117

1009
1·262

1013
1·256

1740
2·066

·424

1011
·306

1012
·615

1733
6·871

1742
4·008

1743

1·782

Knilly Wood

1·051

1734
·005

Causeland station with a down train arriving in the charge of No. 4569.
Hugh Davies

Taken from the 25-inch Ordnance Survey for 1907. (Crown Copyright reserved)

discernible from the platform, as it is entirely surrounded by trees, and not even railed in.'

Causeland was the only intermediate station when passenger services commenced between Moorswater and Looe in 1879. Its appearance has probably changed little over the 115 years of its existence although the wooden platform wall was rebuilt in masonry sometime during the GWR era. As well as the shelter, the only other items on the platform were two oil lamps. At the Looe end of the platform, a track crossed the line on the level, giving access, via a bridge over the East Looe River, to the meadow opposite the station. This track was gated from the lane and also allowed passengers access to the platform.

Only a farm stands in the vicinity and it is difficult to understand why a station should have been provided here. However, when Sandplace station opened in 1881, and St. Keyne opened in 1902, closure of Causeland was proposed

on both occasions but petitions from local residents were received and the station remained open. The present owners of the farm, just to the south of the station, have landscaped an area around the station to complement their holiday accommodation business and Causeland currently presents a tidy appearance.

Down trains pulling away from Causeland would do so with gusto, the falling gradient of 1 in 199 favouring the locomotive, and the engine exhaust, particularly from the 45XX class, would echo off the surrounding hillsides. The line continued its generally southerly route, wending its way along the valley floor until a side road crossed the line at Plashford Bridge. Originally constructed as an arch of masonry with a span of 12ft, the structure also spanned the course of the old canal. It was numbered three from Looe. Along with the other masonry arches on the line, it, too, was rebuilt by the GWR to improve the clearances.

An up train arriving at Causeland on 1st July 1956.

R. J. Sellick

A down train pausing at Causeland in the late 1950s. The water level in the adjacent East Looe River indicates that there had been recent heavy rain.
Collection R. S. Carpenter

Plashford bridge, looking north on 7th July 1986.
Author

Tregarland bridge on 17th April 1990, looking towards Liskeard
(*top*) and Looe (*below*).   *Author*

Detail of the supporting
strut of Tregarland bridge
on 17th April 1990.
              Author

SANDPLACE

Sandplace station slumbering peacefully in the sun on 31st August 1954.

R. C. Riley

South of Plashford Bridge the line continues its winding course along the valley until another side road crosses the line. Tregarland Bridge is surrounded by trees and carries the road to Tregarland and Sandplace across both the railway and the East Looe River. Unlike the other overbridges on the line, wrought-iron girders resting on masonry abutments were used for the 18ft span, with additional support from a vertical strut positioned between the railway and the river. Constructed from iron girders riveted together, it seems, from examination of surviving records, that this support was part of the original structure and it begs the question why such a method of construction should have been employed rather than the all-masonry bridges found elsewhere on the line.

Down trains continue on a sweeping left-hand curve for a further 420 yds or so until, after passing beneath another overbridge, they draw up at Sandplace station. When the railway opened for passenger traffic, only the road bridge — the first overbridge on the line from Looe — existed here and it was not until 1881 that a station was provided, opening in September or October of that year. The situation of the station is most picturesque with the surrounding, tree-covered hills all around, the course of the old canal directly opposite the platform and beyond,

the East Looe River, with the masonry bridge spanning railway, canal and river.

The station was provided with a 260ft platform and a timber-clad shelter. Access to the station was from a gate in the fence lining the adjacent road. Around the station are old quarries and disused lime kilns, whilst as the railway curved due south, by a shorter right-hand curve, a row of whitewashed cottages is passed, the last of which served the function of Sandplace Post Office. Beyond the cottages, the valley widened and the small settlement of Sandplace was sited here where the road from Torpoint dropped down into the valley to join the Looe road.

A goods siding was situated directly opposite the village and about 200 yards south of the station, Sandplace being the only intermediate station to be so privileged. Opened in 1879, the siding was double-ended and access from either end was controlled by ground frames (identified, not surprisingly as 'Sandplace Siding North Ground Frame' and 'Sandplace Siding South Ground Frame'), cast-iron plates to this effect being provided by the GWR in May 1909. The siding was about 180ft long and at the time of Mr. Thomas's report in 1901 was laid with rails resting on longitudinal sleepers 'in the GWR old style'. A building – possibly a goods shed – measuring approximately 65ft x 12ft, was

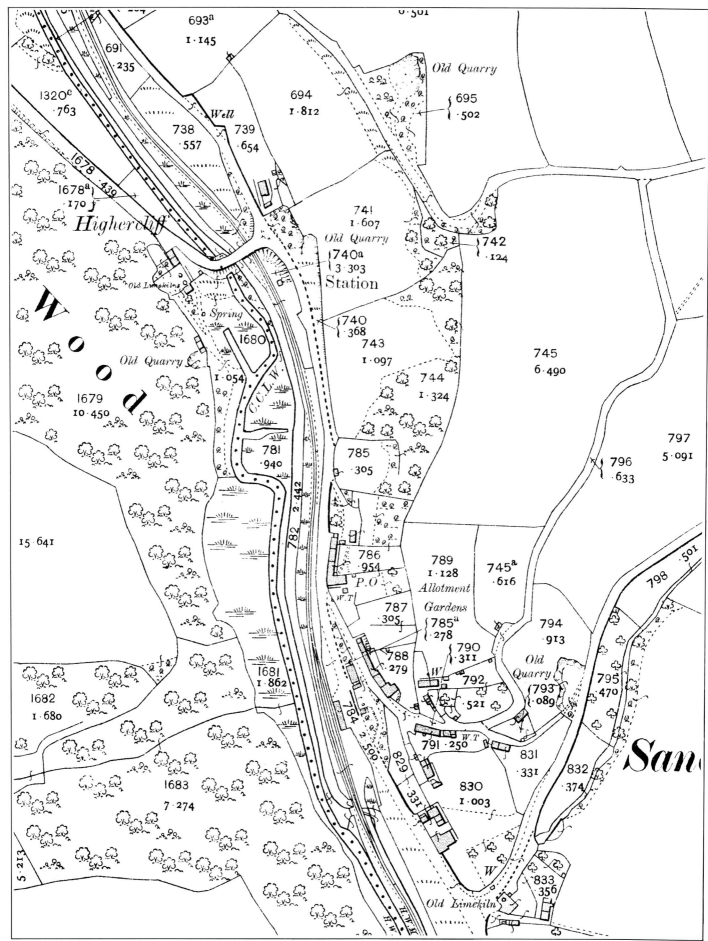

693ᵃ
1·145

Old Quarry
{695
·502

694
1·812

691
235

1320ᶜ
·763

Well

738
·557

739
·654

1678·439

1678ᵃ
170

Highercliff

Old Limekilns

Spring

Old Quarry

1680
1·054

W o o d

1679
10·450

15·641

741
1·607

Old Quarry
{740ᵃ
3·303

Station

{740
·368

743
1·097

744
1·324

742
·124

745
6·490

797
5·091

781
·940

G.C.L.W.

782 2·442

785
·305

796
·633

1682
1·680

1681
1·862

786
954

P.O

W.T

789
1·128

Allotment

787
·305

{785ᵃ
·278

Gardens

745ᵃ
·616

794
·913

798·501

1683
7·274

784 2·500

788
·279

790
311

792
·521

W

Old Quarry

{793
·089

795
·470

5·213

829·331

791·250

W.T

San

831
·331

832
·374

830
1·003

W

833
356

Old Limekiln

H.W.M

provided and Holbrook's report of 1905 records that 'a Mr. Edgcumbe had a coal store here'. It is not known whether a loading platform was provided as it has proved impossible to locate any photographs of the siding at any time during its existence. An instruction regarding the loading of timber at Sandplace siding was contained in the GWR Appendix to the Working Timetable which directed that 'as the loading of timber at this place causes the running line to be fouled,

such operation must only be carried out under arrangements made by the District Inspector, who will provide the necessary flagmen'.

Goodman, in his article on the line in the *Railway Magazine* in 1899, placed on record some of the operational details at this wayside station prior to the GWR takeover:

'From Causeland we proceeded at a leisurely rate until we arrived at Sandplace Station, which is built like the last, but it

General view of Sandplace station in September 1961.   *G. Tilt*

Sandplace station waiting shelter c.1950, also showing the timber platform wall which was later rebuilt in concrete blocks.   *C. Gordon Watford*

An up train arriving at Sandplace on 26th May 1957.

R. J. Sellick

appears to be of more importance as the hut possesses a door, and inside was a platelayer's wheelbarrow. Just outside the station is a row of whitewashed cottages, the end one being honoured by a board bearing the words, "Sandplace Post Office", the little village itself being seen to great advantage a little farther on.

'On leaving this station "Kilmar" set up a prolonged whistling; I felt the brakes being applied, and then the train stopped. On looking out, another surprise awaited me. Right on the line in front of us were eight wagons. Had I had a narrow escape of being in a collision on this out-of-the-way line, which had been averted only by the vigilance and presence of mind of those two worthy fellows on the engine? Oh, no; nothing of the kind. As I soon discovered, we were not on the running line at all, but in a siding (goods and coal traffic being dealt with at Sandplace), and here I was a witness of an interesting shunting operation. Having pushed up some of the wagons to enable them to be coupled together, our train backed out of the siding, bringing six of the trucks with it. The guard closed the points, and with the six wagons *in front* of the engine, in addition to those in the rear, we proceeded to the terminal station of Looe, arriving shortly after 4 o'clock.

Closure of Sandplace station, along with the other wayside stations, was proposed in 1907 but was avoided. The station has remained unstaffed throughout its existence, in the GWR era coming under the supervision of the Looe station master. Although probably never heavily used, the

goods siding remained open for traffic until 18th June 1951. It is thought that the connection to the running line at the Looe end of the siding was removed prior to 1939 with access thence only possible at the Liskeard end. It was subsequently removed and today no trace of the siding remains. As with the other intermediate stations, Sandplace remains open to passengers, the experience of peace and tranquillity while waiting for a train here having not changed greatly since it opened.

Sandplace is so named because of the quantities of sea sand dredged at Lantivet and Talland Bays and brought up the Looe river by barge in the days before the canal was built. As recorded elsewhere, there was a canal basin at Sandplace, constructed after the railway was built, and sited near to the goods siding.

South of the station, the line curved sharply to the east, passing the 2-mile post from Looe en route, before making a reverse curve bringing the line again in a southerly direction. The old canal passes beneath the railway several times in this area but the course of the river was diverted to avoid more bridges. At this point, the river has become tidal and, as the valley widens out into the estuary, it soon becomes apparent that journey's end is approaching.

South of Sandplace the valley widens considerably. This view towards Looe on 8th September 1959 shows an up train shortly after passing the down distant signal for Terras level crossing.

R. J. Sellick

This view, taken at 2.40 in the afternoon of 11th July 1959, shows No. 4585 with an extra down passenger train on the sharp curve approaching Terras level crossing. *Peter W. Gray*

TERRAS LEVEL CROSSING

Terras level crossing in September 1961, seen from Terras Bridge.   *G. Tilt*

South of Sandplace, about two miles from Looe, the character of the railway changes dramatically. The narrow, enclosed valley is left behind and, as the East Looe River becomes tidal, an estuary scene of great beauty is laid before the Looe-bound passenger. However, the relationship between the railway and the river is nonetheless intimate for the line is carried on an embankment only feet away from the water's edge. Indeed, so close is the railway to the river that when high spring tides combine with strong onshore winds and heavy rain, the line often floods between Looe and around 2 miles 40 chains, just south of Sandplace.

Flooding was, and remains, a regular occurrence during the winter months and, as the waters rose, a close watch would be kept on the track by the permanent way gang. As soon as the water reached the top of the rail, the train service would be suspended and a bus service substituted for the use of local passengers. After about four hours, the waters would subside sufficiently, but the train service could not be reinstated until the line had been checked by a Permanent Way Inspector and cleared for traffic. It was not unusual for a train to be stranded at Looe and on such occasions the crew would take refuge in the station buildings, the fireman emerging when necessary to keep the boiler of the engine full. Very often ballast would be

washed away as a result of the flooding and the service had to operate at a reduced speed until the permanent way gang attended to the matter.

After the reverse curves south of Sandplace, the line runs straight for a distance of about a third of a mile. To the right of the train, the widening estuary with its mud flats and saltings gives way to steeply rising fields and woods, whilst to the left of the train, the canal contains water but is hardly navigable as the level rises and falls with the tide. Close to the canal bank, the Torpoint road follows the valley down to Looe, whilst the valley side rises steeply away.

A distant signal marked the approach to Terras level crossing and, with the engine whistling to warn the crossing keeper of its imminent appearance, the line curves sharply to the left. The level crossing carries a side road, leading from the A387 Torpoint–Looe road towards Hillhead Cross and the village of Pelynt, across the line. The minor road crosses the estuary by an embankment, with a raised walkway for use by pedestrians at times of high tides. A narrow hump-backed stone bridge carries the road over the river whereupon the road curves sharply to the right and climbs away through Trewith Wood. An old quay and lime kiln stood by the bridge, formerly served by river barges, whilst there are also old quarries in the vicinity of the

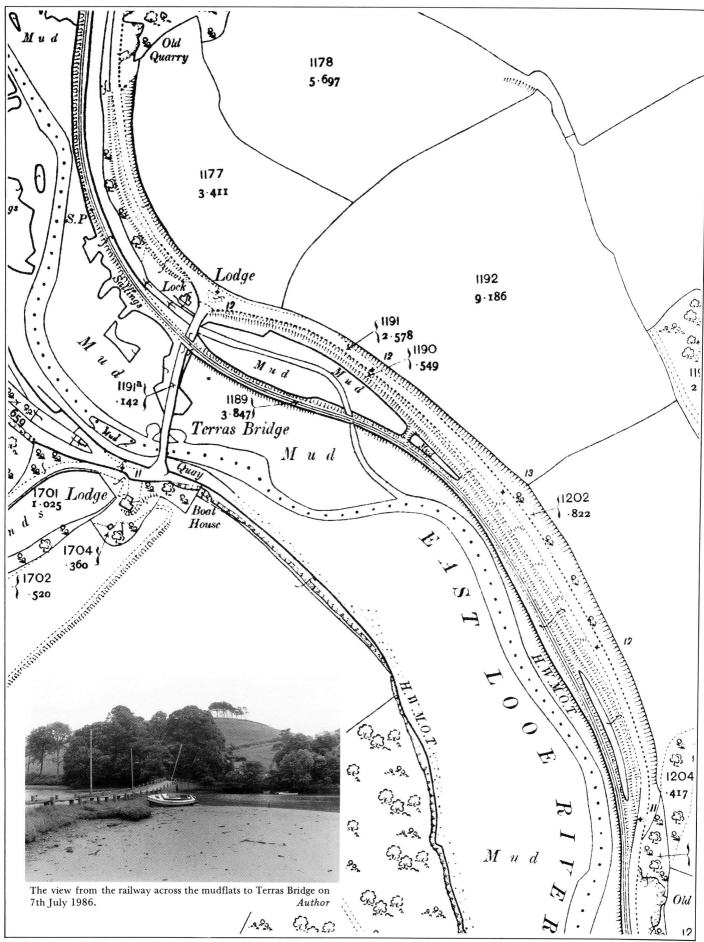

Mud

Old
Quarry

1178
5·697

1177
3·411

1192
9·186

gs

S.P

Lodge

Saltings

Lock

12

1191
2·578

12

1190
·549

1191ª
·142

Mud

Mud

Mud

Mud

1189
3·847

Terras Bridge

M u d

Mud

13

1202
·822

Quay

11

1701 *Lodge*
1·025

n d s

Boat
House

1704
360

1702
520

E A S T   L O O E   R I V E R

T O M W H

T O M W H

M u d

1204
417

The view from the railway across the mudflats to Terras Bridge on
7th July 1986.   *Author*

Old

Taken from the 25-inch Ordnance Survey for 1907. (Crown Copyright reserved)

bridge. To the east of the line, immediately after crossing the railway, the side road crosses the canal by a hump-back bridge before joining the Torpoint road at a 'T' junction.

The level crossing of the railway was protected by heavy wooden gates in the care of a keeper who lived in the adjacent cottage. Distant signals warned trains, approaching the crossing, from either the Looe or Liskeard directions, of the position of the gates and were worked from an open, three-lever ground frame. One lever worked the gate bolt and the other two worked the relevant signals.

Between the railway and the gatekeeper's cottage was the sea-lock which marked the commencement of the canal.

Today the lock chamber is still quite clearly defined and until recent years the remains of the lock-gates were in situ. A ramshackle sluice attempts to control the water level in the old canal, but in practice the water rises and falls with the tides.

The level crossing gates and a cottage for the keeper were provided in 1902. Sited on the bank of the canal, the cottage was occupied by a railway employee until July 1970 when the gates were removed. From the end of the Second World War the keeper was Annie Collins who had joined the GWR during the war as a replacement for male platform staff who had left the railway to join the armed forces.

Terras level crossing seen from an approaching down train in 1959.
J. L. Rapson

The disused sea lock at Terras which gave access to the former canal, photographed in September 1961. *G. Tilt*

The beautiful East Looe River valley on 11th July 1959, with No. 4559 on the 4.40 p.m. from Liskeard approaching Terras level crossing.

Peter W. Gray

On 19th April 1960 No. 4569 had charge of the 11.55 a.m. Liskeard to Looe train seen here below Terras level crossing.   *Peter W. Gray*

Unfortunately, Annie was widowed in the war – her husband had been in the Royal Navy – and when peace came, and most women left the railway service, she took up the gatekeeper's vacancy. She remained at the cottage after the gates were removed until her death. Her daughter also lived in the cottage and was eventually married to Pat Rickard, one of the Moorswater firemen and a regular on the branch service in the 1950s. The gatekeeper's rest days were covered by the Plymouth area relief men and Larry Crozier would often find himself at this idyllic location.

Once the gates had been removed, the crossing was protected by 'stop and proceed' boards erected at the approach to the crossing in both directions. The diesel trains would come to a stand at the board and, having ascertained that no road traffic was near the crossing, would proceed with great caution, making use of the air-horn until the train was on the crossing. This procedure was of particular importance for Looe-bound trains as they approached the crossing by a sharp curve which is shielded from view to road traffic by a stand of trees. Other than the removal of the crossing gates, the location is little changed and the gatekeeper's cottage remains, although now in private ownership.

Beyond the level crossing the line sweeps round to the right, taking the line back into an almost southerly direction. A masonry arch carries the line over the canal for

the last time, at which point the canal physically joins the East Looe River. The railway continues to run in close proximity to the river, elevated above it by an embankment, and when the up distant signal for Terras Level Crossing is passed, the Torpoint road comes in close to the railway to negotiate the next curve in the river.

A high close-boarded fence, erected to stop the trains from frightening horses on the road, separated the road, only feet away from the railway. This fence, covered in a protective coat of bitumen, remained in situ until at least the mid-1920s but the date of its removal is unknown. Having rounded the curve, the railway and road pass Steps Lodge which marks the entrance to the Morval Valley, a side valley off the East Looe River.

At the head of the Morval Valley is Morval House, formerly the home of Buller, the landowner who granted the canal company free use of his land in return for favourable rates for himself and his tenants, when the canal company was experiencing difficulties in obtaining land. The Morval Valley is heavily wooded and the river flow is controlled by a sluice, thus forming a series of lakes used as a freshwater fishery. After passing beneath the road, the outflow from the Morval Valley then passes beneath the railway by means of a stone culvert to join the East Looe River. Adjacent to this culvert and Steps Lodge is the first milepost on the line from the terminus at Looe.

High tide on the East Looe River on 11th August 1951 with Looe visible in the distance.　　　*H. F. Wheeller*

Terras level crossing up distant signal was sited at the point where the Torpoint road comes close to the railway for the last sharp bend in the river before reaching Looe. This view was taken in July 1966.　　　*I. D. Beale*

Near Steps Lodge, the line ran across an embankment over an inlet of the river. This is the view looking towards Looe on 7th July 1986.
Author

The embankment was pierced by a culvert which allowed water from a side valley to drain into the East Looe River. Photographed on 17th April 1990.
Author

No. 5531 with a down passenger train on 9th September 1961 passing the Looe fixed distant signal.

M. J. Messenger

LOOE

At Steps Lodge the train is only one mile from the journey's end. The line continues to run within yards of the widening estuary whilst the Torpoint road keeps company with the railway to a shared destination at the twin towns. Both sides of the valley were formerly wooded, but in recent years the Trenant Woods, on the west side of the river, have been largely destroyed, robbing some beauty from the scene.

After about 800 yards, where the line made a curve to the left following the river bank, the Looe distant signal is passed, marking the final approach to the terminus. The 1907 edition of the 25in:1 mile Ordnance Survey map shows a signal at this point and a replacement was provided by the GWR shortly after the grouping in 1923. The new distant signal was fixed at caution and was mounted on a concrete post. Such signal posts were first used by the GWR during the 1914-18 war and continued in use beyond the grouping, when much resignalling work was required on the newly absorbed lines. Manufactured by Ellis Granite Concrete of Leicester, examples of these posts were to be

The view of Looe station from across the river, with a train arriving at the platform on 1st July 1956.   *R. J. Sellick*

No. 4559 easing its train into the platform at Looe on 18th August 1959.   *P. Hay*

Looe station on 2nd May 1959 with No. 5523 ready to depart with an up train.

R. M. Casserley

An exterior view of Looe station building in the 1960s.
Collection Robert Tivendale

found all over the GWR system but were particularly numerous on the former Cambrian Railways routes in Mid-Wales. The Looe starting signal was likewise mounted on a concrete post.

Beyond the distant signal the line passed the Looe Gasworks, a small establishment set in the bank between the railway and the road. Although the Gasworks was an important customer of the railway, there was no private siding.

Very soon the line rounds a last curve and the train arrives at the single-platformed terminus, having run a distance of 8 miles 54 chains from the starting point at Liskeard. Looe station was sited on the east bank of the Looe River, directly opposite the confluence of the East and West Looe Rivers, in an area known as Shutta. A description of the station in the last years of the 19th century, before the improvement in the line's fortunes following the opening of the connection with the GWR, is found in Goodman's article in the *Railway Magazine* of 1899.

'This station is a counterpart of that at Moorswater, even to the Caledonian time-tables. There is only one signal, which controls trains running to Moorswater. The station occupies a convenient site in the main road of Looe, and from the little platform is obtained a view picturesque in the extreme. Facing is a broad expanse of water flanked by sparsely wooded hills, on the sides of which rises part of the little town from which the station takes its name — an old-world place, "far from the madding crowd's ignoble strife".

'Here our engine was uncoupled, and, leaving the carriages at the platform, took the wagons right down to the harbour, where it was occupied in shunting. The line extends from the passenger station by the side of the harbour for about a mile. It

is separated from the roadway by an iron fence, or rather the remains of one, and there seems to be no objection on the part of the railway company to the public using it as a footpath. It is laid on stone blocks in places, but mostly on longitudinal wooden sleepers.

'The goods yard at Looe, if such it may be termed, is a simple affair indeed. There are no groups of sidings, no points, ground-signals or turntables, no large commodious goods sheds with powerful cranes, but instead there is the one line as it extends from the passenger station across an open space, bounded on one side by the river and on the other by Fore Street (the principal street of Looe). At one end is a large wooden shed used for a miscellany of purposes, and at the other, just before the bridge is reached, is a small coal depot; there are two hand-cranes, by means of which goods may be slung from the railway wagons to the vessels, or vice versa. The extremity of the line passes by some granaries close to the harbour mouth.'

At the time of Goodman's visit, the station building accommodated a booking office and a waiting room with a lavatory. A small wooden goods shed was added at the north end of the building and it is probable that a cast-iron gentlemen's urinal stood on the platform to the south of the building. In preparation for the opening of the 'Extension Railway', a ladies' waiting room had been added, a canopy erected over the platform and the gentlemen's urinal incorporated into a lean-to extension at the south end of the building. In 1901 the station master was H. Hawkes who, employed at a salary of £80 per annum, had come from the Great Eastern Railway along with Holbrook, the Liskeard and Looe Railway's new Traffic Manager.

Although it was extended and altered several times over the years, the original station building at Looe, which dated from the commencement of passenger services in

No. 4585 being watered at Looe on 2nd July 1958. The array of cars in the car park across the river was only a foretaste of what was to come.   *Peter W. Gray*

Covering for the regular Moorswater fireman, relief fireman Jack Truscott of St. Blazey watering his engine at Looe c.1950.
S. J. Dickson

Looe water tank photographed c.1950.

C. Gordon Watford

An up train ready for departure on 1st July 1956. Already cars were being parked in the further extremities of the goods yard.

R. J. Sellick

Expectant passengers waiting while No. 5539 draws their train into the platform on 23rd June 1959.

W. Potter

Looking along the platform at Looe c.1950. The piecemeal extensions to the building over the years are very apparent in this view.

S. J. Dickson

1879, served the town continuously until it was demolished about 90 years later. Along with the improvements to the station building in 1901, the platform was lengthened from 75ft to 200ft to accommodate the longer trains now working over the new line to Liskeard. A signal box was accommodated within the station building between the passenger and goods accommodation, to operate the few signals – which consisted of a starting signal, down distant signal and a home signal. Access to the platform, from the forecourt, was by a gate at the side of the station building, and entry to the booking hall, and other offices and accommodation, was from the platform only.

An elevated tank at the Liskeard end of the platform provided water for locomotives and the 'not drinking water' supply to the station. A masonry tower supported the tank, which had a capacity of 1,661 gallons and was fitted with a 'bag' on a movable jib which delivered water to the tanks of locomotives standing alongside. Beyond the water tank, a loading bank faced onto the running line. Used for loading cattle consigned to and from the adjacent livestock market, it was equipped with a weighbridge and a standpipe for watering the animals and sluicing down the platform.

At the south end of the passenger platform, the running line diverged into three loops, the easternmost serving locomotive and carriage sheds, both constructed of corrugated iron. The locomotive shed measured about 30ft in length

and was provided in 1901 when the revitalised service required a locomotive to be stabled at Looe overnight. The carriage shed measured around 100ft in length and in Longdon's report to the GWR in 1906 he advised that 'the corrugated iron roofs needed attention'.

Having discharged their passengers at the station, passenger trains would draw onto the middle loop to enable the locomotive to run round the coaches using the third loop. There was no facing point lock on the points south of the platform and the working instructions included a strict prohibition to passengers remaining aboard the train as it was drawn into the goods yard. Two goods sidings were provided, one terminating at a carriage shoot, or end loading dock, the other, terminating against the Looe Bridge, being served by an adjacent crane of 2 tons capacity. An extension of the carriage/locomotive shed road ran through a gate to form a line down to the harbour. Before passing through the gate and onto the public highway, the rails traversed a weighbridge, used for weighing trucks consigned to and from the harbour.

After passing across the end of the stone bridge connecting East and West Looe, the harbour line ran over the open expanse of Buller Quay, making its way past the fish market to the quayside beyond. A siding ran along the edge of Buller Quay which was the property of the St. Neots China Clay Co., owners of the dries at Moorswater, and

No. 5572 rolling with its train along the last few feet of its journey in the platform at Looe, on 6th September 1959.

R. J. Sellick

which was connected at either end to the harbour line. This siding was constructed in 1904. All other rails, points and crossings south of Looe Bridge were the property of the Looe Harbour Commissioners but were maintained by the GWR. A store was situated on Looe Quay for the storage of wagon sheets, perhaps used in connection with the china clay traffic.

Beyond the fish market an overhead travelling crane and a large derrick were provided for loading the stone and copper ore, which had travelled down from Cheesewring Quarry and Caradon Hill, aboard sailing vessels tied up at the quayside. Due to limited clearances and tight curvature, locomotives were not permitted to pass these cranes, vehicles requiring movement to and from the farthest extremity of the harbour line being placed by horses.

The harbour line continued for about another 550 feet, along the quayside, before terminating alongside a large three-storey, stone-built warehouse only yards away from

Looe station on 28th June 1948. *R. K. Cope*

The view off the platform towards the river at Looe c.1950. *J. H. Moss*

Shunting activity in the yard at Looe. There was no facing point lock on the point in the foreground, hence the instruction in the Appendix to the Service Timetable which advised that passengers should not remain in trains run into the goods yard for reversing purposes.

J. Norris

the open sea. A pile of sleepers served as a stop block marking the physical end of a line of metals which started thirteen miles away high up on the moors above Liskeard.

It was reported in 1906 that the permanent way, from about 3 miles south of Coombe Junction, consisted of flat-bottom rails spiked to wooden cross sleepers, but that the sidings at Sandplace and Looe needed attention, being 'laid longitudinally (GWR old style)'. By 1909, when the GWR took over working the line, some relaying had been done using bullhead rail in cast-iron chairs resting on wooden sleepers. Very soon the entire line had been relaid in this fashion and only odd lengths of the old flat-bottom rails remained. One such survival was the final length of the quay line to the stopblock which remained thus until it was removed.

Horace Holbrook, the Liskeard and Looe Railway Traffic Manager, issued instructions to enginemen regarding operating procedures at Looe. Due to the lack of facing point locks in the yard, it was required that 'All Drivers of Down passenger trains must stop their engines clear of the Facing Points at Looe end of station platform'. Further, it was advised that 'Tablets to be given up, after train has been brought to stand at the platform'.

Very soon after the commencement of the revised service, resulting from the opening of the connection to Liskeard, problems began with the locomotive water supply at Looe. The storage tank filled too slowly and the railway company were being charged more than double, by Looe Urban District Council, than by their counterparts at Liskeard. In due course a directive was issued by Holbrook that 'only the smallest amount of water be taken at Looe'. As much water as possible was taken at Liskeard and boiler washouts for the locomotive stationed at Looe were henceforth undertaken at Moorswater. In due course, the service was worked entirely from Moorswater, the Looe engine shed closing on 2nd April 1917. The redundant locomotive shed at Looe was sold in 1920.

In 1905 it is recorded that cartage was to be undertaken by the company so that a reliable, regular service in the traffic in small goods could be offered to local traders. A van was purchased for this purpose and the horse was accommodated in a small stable in the station forecourt. The carman was Harry Cox who started with the L & LR in 1902 and transferred to the GWR payroll in 1909. Cartage

No. 4559 drawing its train forward into the yard on 18th July 1960. The bracketed starting signals, shown on the opposite page, had been removed and replaced with ground level disc signals. *R. C. Riley*

Left: Looe signal box c.1950. *Right:* Interior of Looe signal box, showing the 7-lever frame, the diagram and the lamp indicator for the distant signal. *C. Gordon Watford and J. H. Moss*

during the GWR era was by an agent, who used a small Ford lorry, and it was not until nationalisation that the railway authorities again provided their own cartage service. Other staff at Looe in the years before the Great War included Joseph Menhennick, guard; Tom Bowden, signalman porter; Albert Bailey, porter; Fredrick Grant, porter; and William Hannaford, porter.

As the First World War made increasing demands on manpower, women were employed by the GWR to replace men who had left to join the armed forces. A lady porter, Evelyn Burridge, was employed in May 1918 and she remained at Looe until November 1919.

Around 1920 the well-known miniature signal box was provided at the south end of the platform to replace the earlier signalling arrangements within the station building. The new signal box — little more than a wooden cupboard measuring only 5ft by 4ft 6in — accommodated a seven-lever frame and the lamp indicator instrument for the down distant signal. The single-line electric token machine continued to be accommodated in the station building. Additional signalling works undertaken in 1923, once the independent railway was firmly under the wing of the GWR, included the provision of goods starting signals controlling access to the yard and carriage siding. Sited at the top of the ramp at the extreme south end of the platform, the signal had two arms, one on a small post bracketed out from the main post, both arms being of the shorter type employed at such locations. Unlike the other GWR replacement signals at Looe, the post was of timber.

By the 1920s, traffic using the harbour line was largely confined to fish, the granite and china clay traffic at Looe having ceased. Dedicated GWR vehicles were used for fish traffic and were propelled by a locomotive down to the fish market for loading with the catches of herring, mackerel and pilchard. On such occasions the train would be accompanied by two shunters, one of whom was required to walk in front of the moving vehicles to warn the enginemen of any obstruction and to alert any pedestrians of the movements. Fish vans would be stabled on the siding along the edge of the quay, near the fish market, but the siding was otherwise little used and at holiday times the track was frequently covered by the roundabouts and other attractions of travelling fairs.

Although 1923 was the peak year for tickets issued for journeys originating at Looe, increasing numbers of visitors arrived by train as summer holidays by the sea became more popular during the 1920s. To accommodate the additional traffic, the platform was extended to the north in 1928 by 96ft. This took the extended platform beyond the water tank which had to be repositioned further away from the track to allow adequate clearance. Movement of the tank was achieved by the simple expedient of extending the masonry tower at the rear, moving the tank and subsequently demolishing the now unwanted section of the original masonry tower. An extended movable jib arm was required, of course. The new platform extension was constructed with a timber front wall, reinforced with lengths of old Barlow rail, filled behind and surfaced with

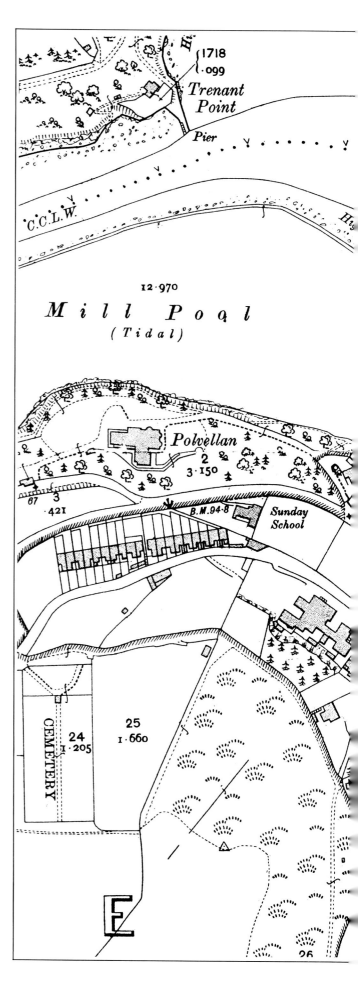

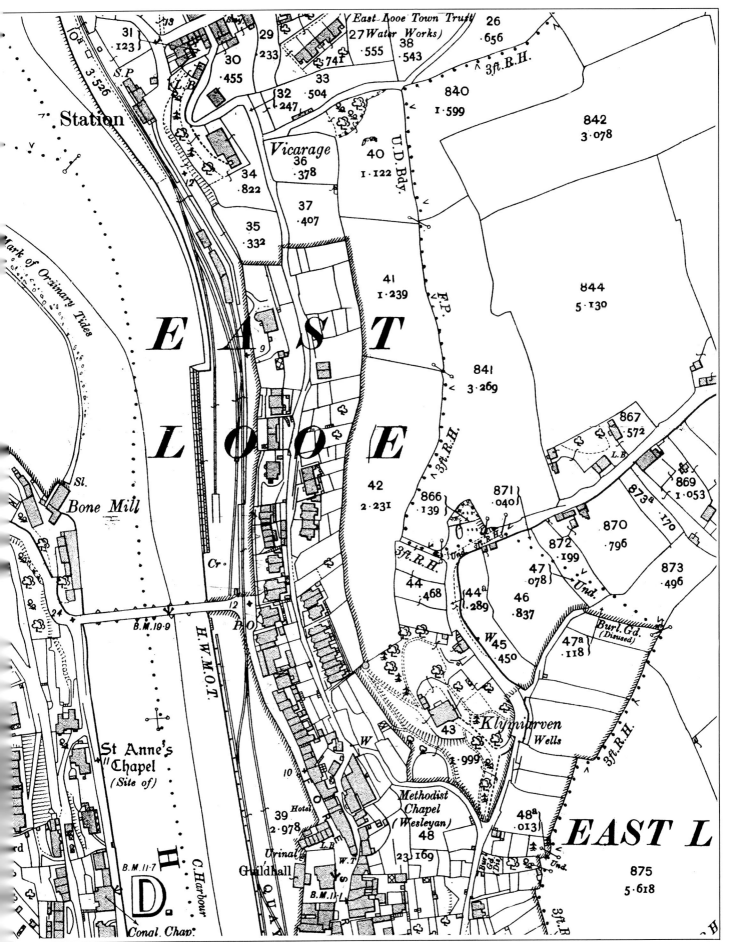

Taken from the 25-inch Ordnance Survey for 1907. (Crown Copyright reserved)

Shunting in progress in Looe goods yard in June 1948.

D. Clayton

ashes. The earlier platform had a masonry front wall and the surface was paved with flagstones around the station building. Also in the late 1920s the old corrugated iron-clad carriage shed to the south of the station was removed.

Passengers arriving at the terminus with heavy hand luggage were greeted by outside porters, as was the custom at many stations. These men were not employed by the GWR, but provided their own barrows and set their own charges. For a small consideration they would accompany arriving visitors to their accommodation in any part of the twin towns, carrying the luggage on their barrow and no doubt hoping for a healthy tip!

In 1934 further improvements to the track layout at Looe were proposed to accommodate the increasing summer traffic. It was planned to lengthen the platform by 40ft at the north end and a further 170ft at the south end, which would necessitate the removal of the 'cupboard' signal box. A new engine run-round loop — 590ft in length between fouling points — was to be provided in front of the platform and the entire station was to be resignalled. The altered layout would be controlled from a new signal box built upon the platform next to the station building, which was to have the canopy extended. However, events referred to in Chapter 3 were likely to have resulted in a new railway to Looe with a newly constructed terminus on an entirely different site. This would have brought about the

closure and removal of the old line from Liskeard, so the improvements did not proceed. Probably for the same reason, a similar scheme, proposed in 1936, also did not proceed. This second plan required extension of the platform at the south end by 280ft, and the provision of an engine run-round loop. The new arrangement would have been controlled from a newly-built signal box sited at the foot of the ramp at the north end of the platform, which was to contain a frame having ten working levers. In both the 1934 and 1936 proposals, the siding capacity in the goods yard was to remain unchanged, reflecting the general decline in goods traffic experienced during the inter-war period. From a high point in 1930, when 28,130 tons were handled, total goods tonnage had declined to 15,689 by 1936 and was to further fall to 14,113 tons by 1938.

Indeed, the only alteration of note during the mid-1930s was the provision of a new hand crane in the goods yard. Although tonnages were declining, the weight of individual consignments must have been increasing because the old 3-ton crane was replaced by a new 6-ton capacity crane of standard GWR design. This work was completed during November 1935.

By 1938, the inadequacies of the facilities at Looe were again making themselves apparent to the staff of the Traffic Department, and proposals for alterations were again made. This time the scheme was of a more modest nature and one detects just a hint of realisation that the new railway might not happen after all as this proposal was proceeded with. So far as the new railway to Looe was concerned, by 1938 very little work had been done other than a detailed survey and some preliminary geological boring, but, according to the surviving records, it should have been fully in operation by 1939 or 1940. The inter-

national situation had changed too, making everything uncertain, and so, whilst no doubt intended as a temporary expedient, the additions to the existing station at Looe went ahead.

In this proposal the track layout was not altered but additional goods and parcels accommodation was provided by extending the existing station building at the north end. The platform verandah covering was extended to the full

No. 5557 drawing its train into Looe yard on 21st June 1956 prior to running round.

Hugh Davies

No. 5534 being recoupled to its train ready for another departure to Liskeard.

Collection R. S. Carpenter

Activity in Looe yard c.1948 with both passenger and goods trains present.   *M. E. J. Deane*

length of the building, which now accommodated, from the north end: goods shed, parcels office, booking office, booking hall, ladies room and gentlemen's lavatory. Brought into use in time for the 1939 summer season, the new accommodation was of great benefit in dealing with the ever-increasing amounts of luggage left by arriving holidaymakers.

Saturdays were traditionally the 'changeover' day and holidaymakers often travelled down to Cornwall overnight. They would arrive by the first or second train down from Liskeard but, as they were not allowed into their hotels or boarding houses until noon, they would often leave their luggage at the Looe station parcels office, paying a modest cloakroom charge for the privilege, and then walk into the town to find breakfast. The parcels office would soon be full to overflowing on these summer Saturdays and in the postwar era the luggage and other parcels were often stacked on the platform. So much was there to be dealt with that the branch train could make a trip to Liskeard and back before the first batch was processed, and yet more would be added to the backlog, from the second train. The parcels office was staffed by a

porter whose duties also included working the signal box while the train drew into the yard for the engine to run round its coaches. During the busy periods, when the porter was fully engaged in the parcels office, the signal box was worked by the fireman of the engine, thus leaving the porter to continue his task uninterrupted. One of the perks of being hard-pressed in the parcels office was that, when the holidaymakers regained their luggage later in the day, they would often give the porter a tip as they were usually generous with their spending money at the beginning of their holiday. In the postwar years it was possible to make £1 or more in this way on a summer Saturday.

The benefits of the increased accommodation were shortlived, however, for the outbreak of the Second World War brought the summer season of 1939 to an abrupt halt. Trippers were not to reappear at Looe again, in appreciable numbers, for another five years, although the hard-pressed residents of Devonport or Plymouth would occasionally take the opportunity for a day out, and Looe was only a short journey away. In the town there was little change although the harbour was protected by a defensive boom laid across the harbour mouth, and two 4-inch guns

The GWR standard 6-ton yard crane provided in 1935, possibly to allow for the increasing use of containers for goods traffic. *S. J. Dickson*

The view from Looe bridge, at low tide, c.1950.

J. H. Moss

Wagons being shunted at Looe c.1950.   *S. J. Dickson*

A shabby No. 4552 in the yard at Looe c.1950. In the background we have a glimpse of the coal wharves used from the mid-1940s by Messrs F. J. Reeves and Alfred Thomas. Access to the wharves for road vehicles was by a sleeper crossing over the siding.   *S. J. Dickson*

LOOE.

A postcard view of Looe, taken in the mid-1930s, showing the full extent of the station and yard and featuring an up passenger train at the platform awaiting departure for Liskeard. The bridge connecting East and West Looe, built c.1848, was designed by William Pease who was also responsible for the Treffry viaduct spanning the Luxulyan valley, on the Cornwall Minerals Railway.

Collection P. Q. Treloar

No. 4568 making its way carefully along the quay line on 17th September 1948 to collect wagons.

mounted. The local boat-building industry was soon engaged on Admiralty contracts, and wooden-hulled mine-sweepers, pinnaces, whalers and cutters were all constructed through the war years, which made a considerable change from the sleek, varnished and painted wooden motor and sailing boats built in the prewar years. So far as the railway is concerned, it seems to have continued about its business affected only by the economies forced upon it by wartime conditions, and no events of any note are recorded.

When peace returned in May 1945, the trippers, too, began to visit Looe again. That first summer was somewhat limited and whilst many hoped to take advantage of the situation to have the break that they had been denied for years, the almost universal retention of rationing meant this was not always possible. One of the first acts of the newly returned postwar Labour government was to nationalize Britain's railways, and on 31st December 1947 the GWR ceased to exist. One of the company's last acts at Looe was to engage a further member of staff who was required in connection with the introduction of the 44-hour working week. The new porter/signalman transferred from Bodmin Road station, but when he actually commenced his employment at Looe, the branch had become part of British Railways (Western Region).

A side effect of the years of war, and the resulting restrictions upon the fishing industry, was that the stocks of fish had a chance to recover, and for a few years in the late 1940s good catches were landed at Looe, from which the railway benefited. On such occasions, all the railway staff, including the engine crews, would assist in loading the fish vans at the quay, and once this task was completed, a box of fish would be sent to the station to be shared out. Within a few years, however, the loaded fish boxes were being sent away more cheaply by road and only the empty boxes were returned by rail as the empties were conveyed free of charge. British Railways soon required that they should convey the loaded fish boxes by rail or they would not convey empty boxes, and consequently carriage of fish by rail from Looe largely ceased.

By the early 1950s, the harbour line was disused and on 23rd March 1954 the decision was made by the Looe Harbour Commissioners to tarmac over the rails. Surprisingly, however, as late as June 1960, the Sectional Appendix to the Working Timetable for the Plymouth Traffic District retained the instruction that 'when an engine or engine and vehicles, is required to go on to the Harbour lines, two shunters must accompany them, one preceeding on foot in front of the engine or engine and vehicles, so that it may be stopped in the event of any obstruction on the line'. In due course, road traffic caused the tarmac covering the rails to wear away, revealing some of the former track layout, to intrigue the present writer when he made his first visit to Looe in 1966. The rails have subsequently been removed and no trace now remains of this distinctive aspect of the railway scene at Looe.

Very little addition to the facilities at Looe was made in the postwar years. Electric lighting was provided in the booking and parcels offices in 1950 but otherwise the station retained its gas lighting. In 1956 the platform was largely reconstructed. The old timber-faced extension of 1928 was removed and rebuilt with concrete blocks and the platform was resurfaced with concrete slabs along the edge of the whole length of the platform and around the station building. At an unrecorded date, access to the platform was altered so that it became necessary for intending passengers to pass through the booking office. A board on the south elevation of the station building, facing passengers arriving from the town, gave notice of this fact. The gate at the south end of the building was used by detraining passengers to avoid congestion in the small booking office, and a GWR notice, of cast-iron letters on a wooden board, advised passengers accordingly.

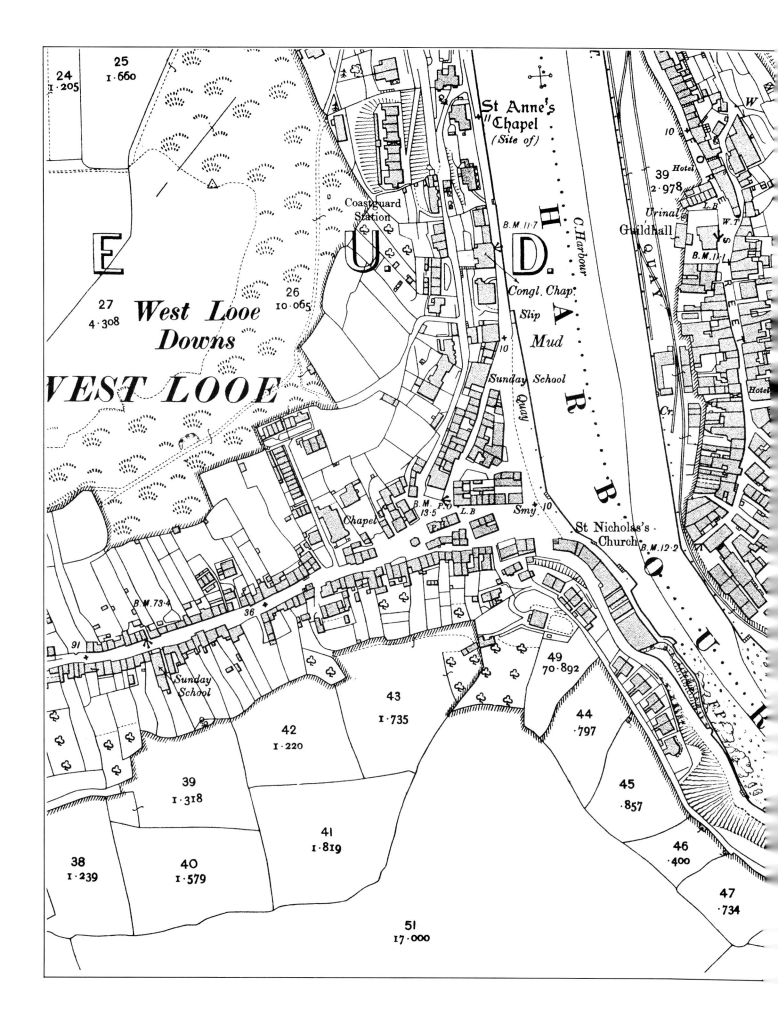

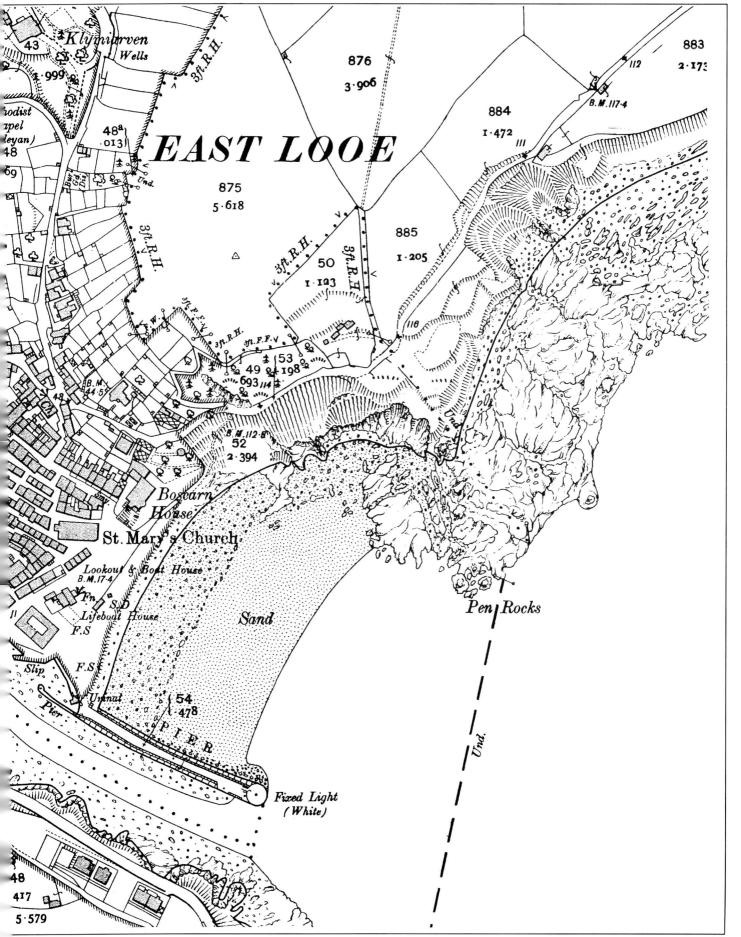

EAST LOOE

Klymiarven
Wells

43

999

48ᵃ
·013

876
3·906

884
1·472

883
2·173

B.M.117·4

112

111

875
5·618

885
1·205

50
1·193

116

53
198

49
693 114

52
2·394

Boscarn
House

St. Mary's Church

Lookout & Boat House

B.M.17·4

Fn S.D

Lifeboat House

F.S

Sand

Slip

F.S

Pier

Urinal

54
478

PIER

Pen Rocks

Und.

Fixed Light
(White)

48

4¹⁷

5·579

Taken from the 25-inch Ordnance Survey for 1907. (Crown Copyright reserved)

As goods traffic at Looe declined, increasing numbers of motor cars made parking in the narrow streets of Looe ever more of a problem and, from about 1955 onwards, the railway authorities allowed car parking in the lightly-used goods yard. A scale of charges was displayed on notices at the station, and posters suggested that motorists should 'park your car at this station and catch a train', thus providing an early example of the now common 'park and ride' schemes. By the early 1960s, barriers, constructed of old bullhead rail, were erected to prevent cars from parking too close to the track as, of course, passenger trains still had to draw into the yard for the engine to run round its coaches. In 1961, however, diesel multiple units replaced steam and there was no longer the necessity for passenger trains to draw into the yard after the passengers had detrained. However, as goods services continued for a few years more, the run-round loop had to be retained until, inevitably, on 4th November 1963, freight traffic ceased to be handled

No. 4561 easing its way across Buller quay c.1950 at a time before car parking in Looe became a problem.

S. J. Dickson

Buller quay on 2nd July 1948 with cars parked on the long-disused china clay siding. By this time only the line across the quay to the fish market remained in use.

R. K. Cope

Looe harbour on 2nd July 1948 with much of the final length of the quay line visible.   *R. K. Cope*

The farthest extremity of the harbour line at Looe on 2nd July 1948. Locomotives were not permitted to pass Morcombe & Co.'s store, although it has not been established precisely where this was. Any wagons requiring to be moved over this section of the line would be drawn by horses.   *R. K. Cope*

at Looe. As if in anticipation of this event, the 6-ton hand crane in the goods yard was taken down and scrapped in August 1963. Car parking in the former goods yard was thus expanded further.

Looe signal box became redundant and closed on 15th March 1964, and the goods sidings and run-round loops were removed. A bufferstop was placed at the end of the line, which was now some twenty yards beyond the end of the ramp, at the south end of the platform. The line was further shortened, by 15 yards, in July 1966 and car parking expanded yet again in the former yard.

On 30th September 1968 the station became unstaffed and the facilities for collection, handing-in and despatch of

freight sundries and parcels at Looe were discontinued. Henceforth tickets were obtained from the conductor/guard on the train, re-booking if necessary at Liskeard for longer journeys. Other facilities such as advance booking of tickets, enquiries, all traffic labelled 'To be called for', and parcels and freight sundries traffic were transferred to Liskeard station. The station buildings were subsequently demolished and now only a small waiting shelter is provided at Looe for intending passengers. To the south of the station, the land formerly occupied by the goods yard was sold by British Railways, to Cornwall County Council, and in recent years a petrol filling station and a police station have been built on the site.

View north from Lamellion bridge, on 2nd August 1958, towards Moorswater with a 'Hall' class 4—6—0 crossing the viaduct on the 6.27 a.m. (Saturdays only) Falmouth to Plymouth train.

Peter W. Gray

MOORSWATER

Looking along the line towards Moorswater on 23rd June 1950, a view not greatly changed to the present day. *R. K. Cope*

After the opening of the connecting line from Coombe Junction to Liskeard in 1901, the railway north of Coombe reverted to goods only traffic. Immediately to the north of the newly provided Coombe Junction station and signal box stood Lamellion Bridge — named after the neighbouring hamlet — and this original structure of 1859 was not rebuilt by the GWR as were all the masonry overbridges south of Coombe to Looe. Lamellion Bridge remains in its original condition to this day, its limited clearances apparently not causing any problems to the working of the small amount of clay traffic still originating from Moorswater.

Access to the line north of Coombe was under the control of Coombe Junction signal box. A shunting signal was provided to allow entry to the goods line whilst strict instructions governed the working of goods trains to and from the old line and of light engines running to and from Moorswater engine shed. The GWR Appendix to the Working Time Table for the Plymouth Area, dated 'May 1919 Until Further Notice' read thus:

Coombe Junction and Moorswater — No Engine or Train may pass between Moorswater and Coombe Junction North End, unless the Driver is in possession of a Train Staff.

When an Engine or Train is leaving Coombe Junction for Moorswater and is not returning to Coombe, arrangements must be made by the Engineman for a Fireman, Guard, or Engine Cleaner to return the Staff to the Signalman at Coombe Junction if it is likely to be required for another Engine to travel from the direction of Coombe.

If the Engine is shortly returning to Coombe Junction, the Staff may be retained at Moorswater, and will be authority for it to do so.

The disused piers of Brunel's timber viaduct at Moorswater in August 1978. *M. J. Mitchell*

Looking south down the East Looe River valley on 22nd April 1957 from a train crossing Moorswater viaduct. Lamellion bridge with Coombe Junction beyond can be seen in the middle distance.
R. J. Sellick

Moorswater yard on 27th May 1956 from a train crossing the viaduct. The loaded china clay wagons on the loop were waiting to be weighed.
R. J. Sellick

While the Staff is away from Coombe Junction no Engine or Train may pass beyond the North Junction at Coombe Platform towards Moorswater.

At night (or when not in use at Moorswater during the day) the Train Staff must be locked up in the Box provided for the purpose, in the Engine Shed at Moorswater.

The Signalman at Coombe Junction will be responsible for the working of the Staff between the time it is handed him by the first Engine or Train in the morning, until he hands it over to the last Engine at night.

The Engine Driver working the last Engine to Moorswater at night will be held responsible for seeing that the Staff is duly locked up in the box provided in the Engine Shed at Moorswater.

In 1921 train staff working was done away with and the line north of Coombe came to be worked as a 'Yard'. Operating instructions were considerably simplified, the Appendix to the Working Timetable for 1939 reading:

Coombe Junction and Moorswater

The line between Coombe Junction and Moorswater is worked as a Yard. Drivers must regard the lowering of the Signal to enter the Moorswater Yard only as an indication that the points are in the proper position, and must not expect that the road will be clear through the Yard, and they will be held responsible for stopping their trains short of any obstruction which may be in front of them.

Whilst in the Yard after dark, all engines must carry a red head light.

The wording remained substantially the same until well into the 1960s.

North of Lamellion Bridge the railway runs to Moorswater alongside the course of the old canal, the remains of which once again became apparent, having been obliterated in the region of Coombe Junction by the construction of the Liskeard and Looe Extension Railway. A footpath from Lamellion to Moorswater also accompanies the railway which by now is dominated by the majesty of the Moorswater Viaduct. This structure crosses the valley, carrying the Cornwall Railway main line in an east-west direction, the metals of which pass 147ft above those of the Liskeard and Caradon Railway. As recorded elsewhere, the original fragile timber structure of Brunelian design was replaced in 1880-81 by the double-track masonry viaduct which continues in use to the present day. As late as the 1930s, and possibly even until 1936, the section of line from Coombe to Moorswater was constructed of old flat-bottom rails spiked to wooden sleepers. In due course it was reconstructed with standard GWR bullhead rails resting in cast-iron chairs.

The old Liskeard and Caradon Railway Moorswater station was situated within the shadow of the Moorswater viaduct and very slightly to the north of it. This station was

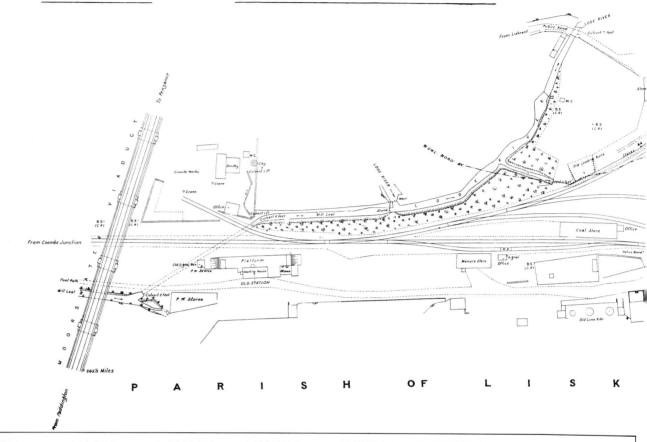

Looking south across Moorswater yard on 23rd June 1950. This view was taken from the side road that crossed the site from the A38 road.

R. K. Cope

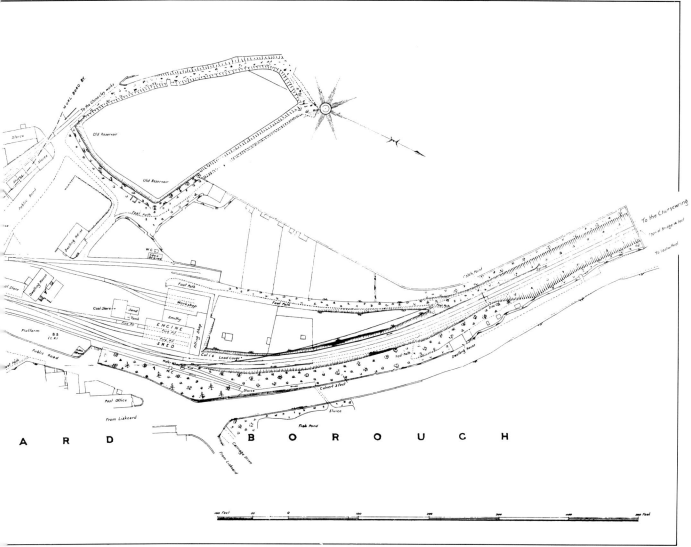

erected on the site of the first lock on the old canal and formed the upper terminus for passenger working by the Liskeard and Caradon Railway. Again Goodman provides a graphic description of the site from his visit to the line in 1898:

'I crossed the Great Western bridge, and, following the road for a short distance, came to a guide-post bearing the words, "To Moorswater Station". Turning off in the direction indicated, I went along a typical Cornish road, narrow, winding and steep — so steep that a stranger is surprised to see horses taking loads up and down with comparative ease. Still plodding on, I found another guide-post similar to the first, and eventually found myself close to a footpath, which led to my destination. Entering by a swing gate, and proceeding along this path gave me an opportunity of examining the permanent-way of this interesting little railway. Hereabouts the sleepers were in reality stone blocks about 2ft 6in square, to which the rails were fastened by large nails. There are no telegraph wires, nor is the line fenced in at all; it is a single line of the standard gauge, and, being worked by "one engine in steam" only, no train staff or electric tablets are necessary.

'I soon reached Moorswater Station, and, having about half an hour to wait before the departure of the train, devoted the time to a survey of the place. The platform is about ten yards long, built of blocks of granite, with a sleeper border, and covered with a layer of tarred granite chippings. The station buildings consist of a white painted wooden structure with a galvanised iron roof, which is divided into two spaces, one being occupied by the booking-office and the other by a general waiting-room. At one end is the lavatory accommodation, and at the other a diminutive goods shed. On the outside of the waiting-room is exhibited a large notice-board on which appear the conditions subject to which *free passes* are issued by the Company, but more surprising still is a large board with the Caledonian Railway's current time-tables posted thereon.

'A few feet off is a rude shelter constructed of zinc, under which goods can be transferred from carts to the railway wagons, while farther still is the little water tank, coal store, and an engine and carriage shed combined. Almost above head is Moorswater Viaduct, under which the line passes. For shunting purposes and general terminal station work, two or three sidings are quite sufficient, while there is also a small signal-box containing the necessary levers for working one set of points and

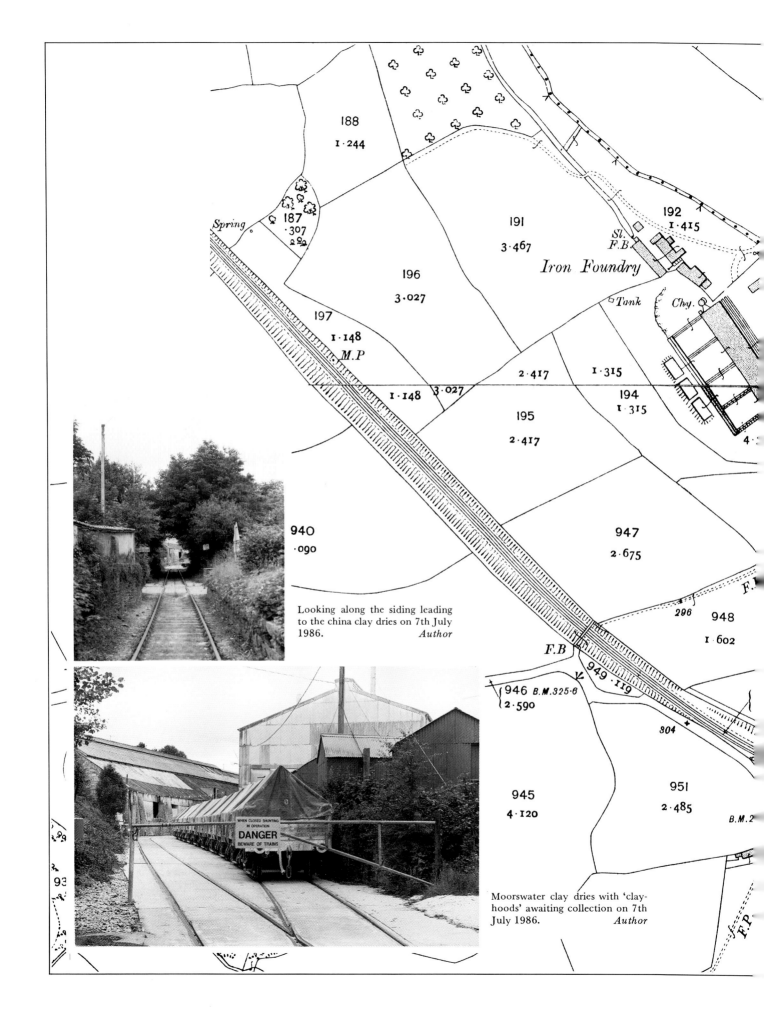

188

1·244

187
·307

Spring

191

3·467

196

3·027

192
1·415

Iron Foundry

St.
F.B

Tank

Chy.

197

1·148

M.P

1·148   3·027

2·417   1·315

194
1·315

195

2·417

4

940

·090

Looking along the siding leading
to the china clay dries on 7th July
1986.   *Author*

947

2·675

F.

296   948

1·602

F.B

949 ·119

304

DANGER
BEWARE OF TRAINS
WHEN CLOSED SHUNTING
IN OPERATION

946 B.M.325·6

2·590

945

4·120

951

2·485

B.M.2

Moorswater clay dries with 'clay-
hoods' awaiting collection on 7th
July 1986.   *Author*

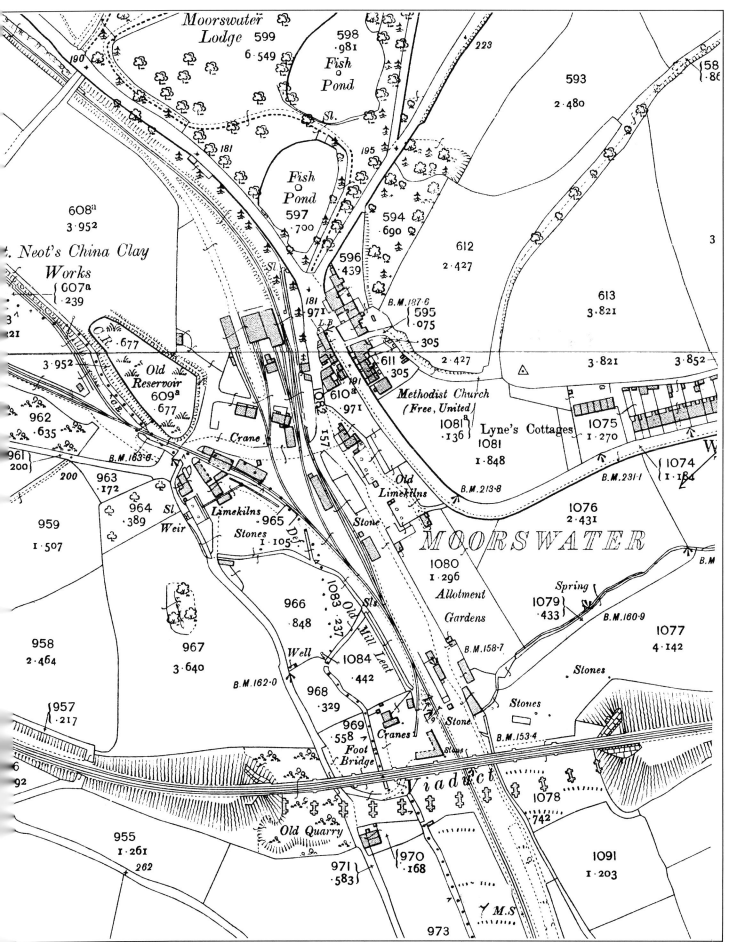

Moorswater
Lodge 599
598
·981
6·549
223

Fish
Pond

593
2·480

58
·86

190
181

195

3

t. Neot's China Clay
Works

608ᵃ
3·952

607ᵃ
·239

Fish
Pond
597
·700

594
·690

612
2·427

613
3·821

21

3·952

596
·439

B.M.187·6
595
·075

181
971

L.B

305

611
305

2·427

3·821

3·852

Old
Reservoir
609ᵃ
·677

C.R. ·677

610ᵃ
971

157

Methodist Church
(Free, United)

1081ᵃ
·136
1081
1·848

Lyne's Cottages

1075
1·270

962
·635

Crane

W

B.M.163·6

961
200

B.M.231·1

1074
1·184

963
·172

964
·389

Sl.
Weir

Limekilns
965
·105

Old
Limekilns

B.M.213·8

1076
2·431

MOORSWATER

959
1·507

Stones
1·105

Stone

1080
1·296

Spring

B.M.

B.M.160·9

966
·848

1083
·237

Old Mill Leat

Stone

Allotment

Gardens

1079
·433

1077
4·142

958
2·464

967
3·640

Well

B.M.162·0

1084
·442

B.M.158·7

Stones

Stones

B.M.153·4

957
·217

968
·329

969
·558

Cranes

Stone

1078
·742

6

92

Foot
Bridge

955
1·261

262

971
·583

Old Quarry

Viaduct

970
·168

1091
1·203

M.S

973

The former Moorswater station building in April 1949 when it served as a dwelling for the overnight shedman. The building has since been demolished but a visit to Moorswater on 30th May 1995 revealed that the former platform is still visible.   *Author's collection*

what few signals are needful. The signalling arrangements are of the simplest, consisting of two signal-posts, each carrying two arms controlling incoming and outgoing (they can hardly be termed *up* and *down*) trains. In the station are two sets of rails, which converge into a single line a short distance away. Block working, of course, there is none.'

As the station described above closed on 15th May 1901 — on the same day that the new line from Coombe Junction opened for traffic — very few other details of it have survived. The small signal box described had a stone-built locking room with a timber-built upper section accommodating the operating floor and the structure had a slate-covered hip roof.

The 'few signals' consisted of two pairs of arms mounted on two 20ft high signal posts. Up trains were controlled from a post sited just south of the Moorswater Viaduct, the upper arm being for goods and mineral trains and the lower for passenger trains. The second signal post was opposite the station platform, the upper arm being the starting signal for passenger trains and the lower for down goods and mineral trains. Catch points were interlocked with the signals and a distant signal was sited south of Moorswater station.

Although Goodman's article gives a length of ten yards, the 1907 edition of the Ordnance Survey 25-in map reveals that the platform was about 84ft in length, the ramps being about 10ft in length. The main station building measured about 30ft by 15ft. Following the closure of Moorswater station, the track in front of the platform was removed but the former station building was retained and converted to provide living accommodation for railway employees. In 1944 it was recorded that 'the site and raised platform can

clearly be traced and a bungalow type residence forming part of the old station building is used by the man who carries out night duties at the engine shed'. The structure was certainly in evidence in 1949 but does not now exist.

Directly opposite the former passenger station a private siding led to a stone-dressing yard owned by the Cheesewring Quarry Co. where stone was cut by hand and polished by steam power. It is not known when the yard was established or when the siding was provided, but in later years — possibly after Cheesewring Quarry ceased work — the yard passed into the ownership of Cornwall County Council. By the early 1960s the siding had not been used for a considerable time and the private siding agreement was terminated on 7th January 1964, the track being removed and the junction made good at the council's expense.

Immediately beyond the former passenger station, the tracks diverged into a number of sidings, thus forming the 'neck' of the yard. In the same position the former canal had diverged into two arms, providing sufficient wharf frontage to permit loading the large quantities of ore being conveyed down from Caradon Hill and the equally large quantities of coal travelling in the reverse direction. The water level was maintained by a reservoir, supplied by a leat, which had been provided to maintain a good supply of water to the canal at times of heavy traffic. Around the quays were coal and lime stores as well as yards for the storage of copper ore and granite. Along either side of the valley were a number of lime kilns, some of which were supplied from the canal by plateways, the inclines of which were powered by waterwheels. These lime kilns were at work for very many years and in 1961 a former employee of the L & LR recalled that when he joined the railway staff in 1905, 'lime burning was still going on at Moorswater and the yard was full of great heaps of coal'. He also recalled that 'farmers came to the yard for lime and manure'.

When the railway from Caradon was built, it ran down the east side of the valley to terminate at Moorswater alongside the head of the canal where ore yards were established. One siding ran over the canal basin, to permit ore to be discharged into canal vessels through the bottom doors of wooden chauldron-type wagons which had run down from Caradon by gravity. A cottage was demolished to allow construction of the railway, and within ten years of opening, additional sidings and storage capacity had been provided.

Construction of the railway to Looe transformed the facilities at Moorswater as the railway was largely built over the site of the canal. Introduction of locomotive power brought the requirement of an engine shed and this was erected about 1863 and was extended in 1878. In 1909 the GWR surveyed the locomotive shed and reported that the structure was of stone, measuring internally 64ft x 32ft and had a gable roof of slates laid on battens. The shed contained two tracks, that on the left-hand side accommodating the running road whilst the right-hand track was used for engine repairs. Each track had an inspection pit between the rails measuring 59ft 3in in length. Outside the shed was a pair of sheerlegs used for the running repairs of locomotives, although these are recorded as 'rotten' in 1909. At the rear of the engine shed was a fitting shop, measuring internally 49ft by 12ft, and containing a 9-inch lathe, shaping machine, Whitworth pillar drilling machine, screwing machine and two small foot lathes. Power for this machinery came from a waterwheel.

At the front of the engine shed stood a water tank, mounted on a stone base, measuring 8ft x 8ft x 7ft 6in and having a capacity of 2,800 gallons. Water to supply the tank was lifted by a waterwheel and was extracted from the ornamental lakes of a house known as Moorswater Lodge which in turn were supplied by natural springs. To supple-

No. 5519 shunting wagons, including a 'Bloater' fish van bound for Looe, at Moorswater yard. *J. Lowe*

Shunting in progress at Moorswater on 27th August 1936.

R. K. Cope

The wagon weighbridge and hut with old lime kilns behind. This location has been transformed by the construction of the Liskeard bypass road.

Collection R. S. Carpenter

Moorswater on 27th August 1936 with the side road from the A38 in the foreground. The water tank and coal stage outside the engine shed feature on the right whilst the chimney at the china clay dries can be seen in the centre and, to the left, the ruins of former cottages.

R. K. Cope

ment the waterwheel, the pump could be operated by steam power, the supply for which was delivered via a flexible pipe, from an adjacent locomotive.

Between the water tower and the engine shed building was a coal store and loading stage. Constructed of timber on a stone foundation, this structure measured 20ft by 25ft 3in. Between the rails of the track immediately in front of the coaling stage/water tank, was a pit, measuring 29ft in length, used for the preparation and disposal of locomotives. In 1909, Waister's report records that 'all buildings are in good repair and the tools, plant and machinery well cared for', although it 'has not been found practicable to increase the lighting of the shop where the locomotives are repaired although it is desirable'.

In 1909 Moorswater was used to stable the engines used on the mineral trains, the passenger engine being stabled overnight at Looe. Maintenance, boiler washouts, etc., for all the locomotives was carried out at Moorswater, however.

To the west of the engine shed was a wagon repair shop containing two tracks and formerly used for maintenance of the independent railway's rolling stock. Measuring 44ft by 27ft, the shop had a wooden front elevation, and at the rear were stores and a paint shop. Between the engine shed and the wagon repair shop was a smith's shop, with a double hearth, which provided blacksmithing for both loco-

motive and wagon repairs. All these facilities, essential to the independent railway, were soon simplified by the GWR and the wagon repair shop and other shops became disused.

One of the rooms at the back of the engine shed was used latterly by the enginemen as a mess room cum store room whilst engine lamps and the oil supply were kept in another room. From time to time the Permanent Way Department used one of the disused shops for storing tools and materials. During GWR and BR days, apart from routine maintenance, adjusting brakes and the like, all repairs and washouts were undertaken at the St. Blazey parent shed, the engines being changed every fortnight.

The former route to Caradon passed close by the east side of the engine shed. When the track was removed late in 1916, a short section was left in situ to serve as a head-shunt for goods trains shunting in the yard, and occasionally wagons would be stored at the far end of the truncated line. One of the features for which Moorswater is well known was the wrapper of an old locomotive firebox which, fitted with wooden doors and spanning a stream, served for many years as a lavatory for railway employees. Sited opposite the engine shed, the firebox is reputed to have come from *Caradon* which had been withdrawn in 1907.

South of the engine shed, a public road crossed the site and when shunting was in progress in the yard, the goods guard was required to stand on the crossing to warn any road traffic of the moving engine or wagons. Adjacent to the road crossing was a loading platform, disused in later years, whilst to the south of the crossing a loop off the running line accommodated a weighbridge. An instruction in the GWR Appendix to the Working Timetable warned that 'The weighbridge road at Moorswater must not be used as a running road' as the passage of a locomotive across the weighbridge would severely damage the weighing machine.

From the neck of the yard another siding led off to the west of the site to serve china-clay dries. The dries were established in 1902 by the St. Neots China Clay Co. and were supplied with liquid clay, extracted nine miles away at Parsons Pit on Bodmin Moor, and piped to Moorswater. Construction of the dries and the siding required the diversion of a stream into a culvert whilst four trucks of stone per day were brought down from the quarry at

Moorswater water tank in 1958. *S. J. Dickson*

No. 5573 resting at Moorswater in September 1961, at the end of the early turn, with the enginemen making their way home. *G. Tilt*

No. 5553, on 7th August 1961, inside the shed at Moorswater at the end of the early turn. The engine crew had just cycled off and left the photographer alone with the engine still in light steam. *P. Barnfield*

Moorswater on 12th June 1934 with the carriage shed on the left and the workshop, centre, that was shared with the locomotive shed. The rear of the coal stage features in the right foreground with the water tank and engine shed beyond. The carriage shed and workshop were largely disused following the GWR takeover of the L & LR.   *L & GRP*

Moorswater engine shed in 1952 by which time the coal stage had disappeared, the engines being coaled directly from a wagon stabled at the back of the engine shed.   *P. J. Garland*

Cheesewring for use in the new works. Once the ground for the siding had been made up to formation level, by the St. Neots Clay Co, the track was laid by the 'professional platelayers' of the Liskeard and Looe Railway Co. at the expense of the Clay Company. Six trucks of sand per week were also brought down from East Caradon to Moorswater for construction purposes.

The clay dries were completed by 1904 and the first consignment was shipped from Looe in November of that year, a siding having been provided on Buller Quay at the Clay Company's expense. In due course, the dries passed into the ownership of H. D. Pochin and Co., whilst in 1932 the principal china clay producers amalgamated to form English Clays, Lovering, Pochin & Co. Ltd., usually known as ECLP. The dries remain in production to the present day and are still served by rail, the only track now remaining at the site.

As well as the structures already described, a number of timber-framed and corrugated-iron-covered sheds were established but, due to their light construction, few details survive. The records reveal that in 1887 'two sheds be erected at Moorswater at a cost not exceeding £80'. Payments for timber and a 'circular iron roof' are noted. The date of their demise is unknown but an early photograph shows their position, whilst the GWR survey of 1909 reveals that they served as coal stores. Indeed, the minutes also tell us that locomotive coal was purchased every six months and stored, possibly in these sheds, at Moorswater. It is likely that the sheds were removed by the GWR along with the general reduction of facilities at Moorswater following the takeover.

By the 1920s, Moorswater's principal function was to provide locomotive power to work passenger and goods services on the Looe branch, serving as a sub-shed of St. Blazey. Two locomotives and three engine crews were stationed there, two crews to work the passenger service and one to work the goods duty. In addition there was a shed labourer/cleaner who worked at the shed overnight on disposal and preparation duties. He also coaled the engines, lit the fire in the morning (or kept the fire in overnight) and cleaned the engines when not otherwise occupied. The china clay dries continued to provide the majority of traffic originating from Moorswater.

The main A38 Bodmin—Liskeard road passed close by the site and even in the 1930s was causing problems to traffic due to the sharp curvature and narrowness of the carriageway. As early as 1936 proposals were made for a new dual carriageway to pass within feet of the engine shed and, using the course of the former Caradon line to Looe Mills, to continue on to Lostwithiel. The new road would have required the demolition of a number of nearby cottages but the scheme did not proceed, neither did a

Looking south in September 1961 from alongside the engine shed and showing the truncated stub of the former Liskeard and Caradon Railway, which remained in use as a headshunt for the yard.   *Collection Robert Tivendale*

Right: The former locomotive firebox, reputedly from *Caradon* which was withdrawn from service in 1907, used as a lavatory for railway staff at Moorswater. Photographed on 18th July 1960.
R. C. Riley

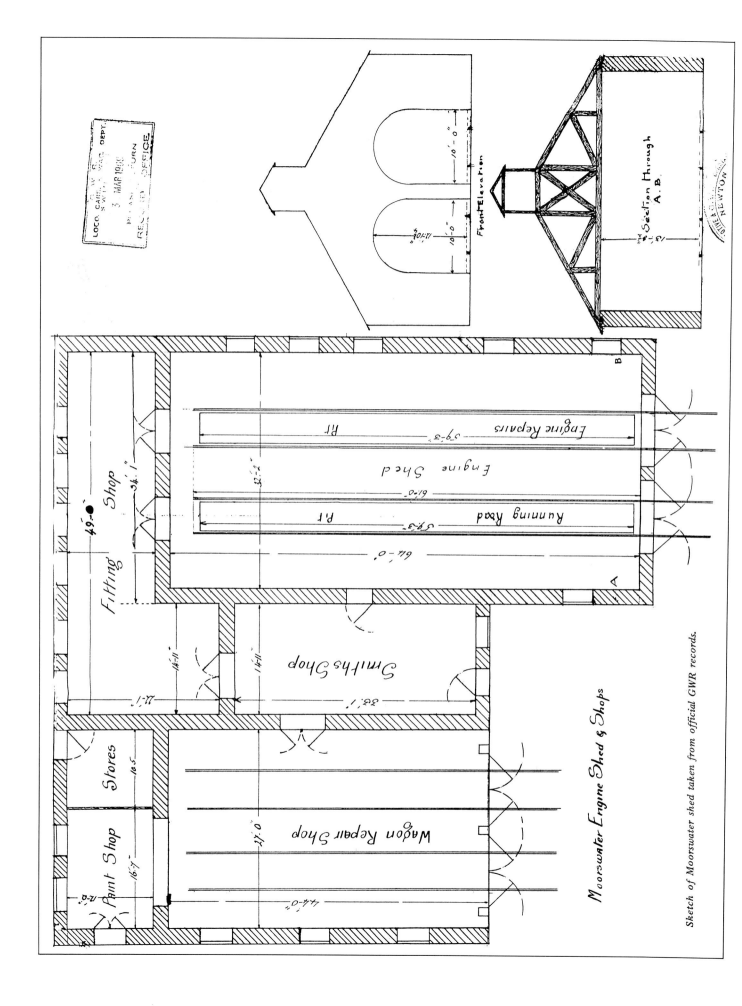

Front Elevation

10'-0"

10'-0"

10'-0"

11'-10⅜"

Section Through A.B.

13'-1"

J.W. SHEARMAN del.
NEWTON.

Fitting Shop

34'-1"

49'-0"

32'-2"

Engine Repairs — 59'-3" —
Engine Shed
61'-0"
Running Road — 59'-3" — R.t
61'-0"

R.t

B

A

Stores

Paint Shop

10'-5"

16'-7"

12'-0"

Smiths Shop

14'-11"

14'-11"

12'-1"

38'-1"

Wagon Repair Shop

17'-0"

44'-0"

Moorswater Engine Shed & Shops

Sketch of Moorswater shed taken from official GWR records.

similar proposal made in 1939. Indeed, it was 1974 before a new road was constructed, but by this time the site at Moorswater was of little use to the railway.

The engine shed closed on 11th September 1961 when steam ceased on the branch, and by 1966, when the writer visited the site, the track into the engine shed had been removed but the buildings were otherwise intact. Demolition came in 1969 and the subsequent construction of the Liskeard Bypass, as well as the establishment of an industrial estate, has transformed the site, with little remaining of the canal or railway. Only the clay works remains and is still served by rail. The route from Coombe Junction is unchanged but, after passing beneath the viaduct, the line becomes double, to form a run-round loop, before curving to the west to run directly into the clay dries.

Rear elevation of the locomotive shed (left), workshop (centre) and carriage shed (right) in September 1961. Apart from one room used to keep the engine lamps and oil supply, the rooms at the back of the sheds were deserted.   *Collection Robert Tivendale*

View south towards Moorswater from the A38 road on 27th August 1936. The truncated stub of the former L & CR can just be seen in the centre of the photograph with the engine shed beyond.   *R. K. Cope*

'County' class 4-6-0 No. 1023 *County of Oxford* arriving at Liskeard with the 12.5 p.m. Plymouth to Truro train on 11th July 1959, while passengers on the opposite platform were gathering for an up train which had already been signalled.

Peter W. Gray

POSTWAR AND NATIONALIZATION

AFTER six long years of war, the branch was able to regain its increasingly important function of transporting trippers and holidaymakers. The summer of 1945 was relatively quiet with many wartime restrictions and rationing still in force, but in 1946 things really began to take off. As a sign that normality was returning, the traditional excursions from Plymouth by sea and rail resumed when in April the *Sir John Hawkins* returned to railway service and duly appeared off the harbour mouth at Looe. She had been extensively refitted following her wartime duty with the Admiralty at Scapa Flow. Her sisters *Sir Francis Drake* and *Sir Richard Grenville* returned to GWR service later in 1946 and, as well as tendering duties at Plymouth, both resumed their excursion work. As an indication of the numbers of passengers carried on these popular excursions immediately after the war, it is recorded that the steamers *Sir John Hawkins* and *Sir Richard Grenville* brought 365 and over 800 passengers respectively from Plymouth in two days alone. The latter then took 363 passengers for a trip from Looe to the Eddystone lighthouse. The railway, of course, had played its part in trans-

porting these visitors to and from the area, the infrastructure remaining largely unchanged from prewar days even if the locomotives and rolling stock were still painted in the dowdy, austerity paint schemes of wartime.

On 1st January 1948 the Looe branch found itself in the brave new postwar world of the nationalized railway system, the Liskeard and Looe branch becoming part of the Western Region of British Railways. Changes were few at first but in due course the engines and coaches began to appear in new corporate liveries. With the ending of the austerity measures throughout the country and the impact of the Holidays with Pay Act at last being felt, in the summer months at least the branch was entering its busiest ever period. One interesting development at Looe in the postwar years was shark fishing as a popular pursuit and the establishment of the town as its principal base. So popular did it become that in due course every available boat in the harbour was employed and the Shark Fishing Club of Great Britain was established with its offices in Looe.

But in spite of the return of the holiday trade, an important source of income for both town and railway, the old

No. 4554 arriving at Looe with another train from Liskeard.   *Author's collection*

No. 5553 being prepared for the early turn at Moorswater in September 1961. The late-turn engine was still inside the shed and would be prepared for service later.

R. J. Sellick

order was changing. On 1st September 1953 *Sir Francis Drake* made her last excursion to Looe and was withdrawn from service soon afterwards. The vessel was not replaced and although her two remaining sisters continued to call, the local excursion trade was in terminal decline from the mid-1950s onwards. On the railway, business apparently continued to flourish as the postwar boom in tourism grew ever larger, although escalating operating overheads were beginning to ring warning bells at the highest levels of BR management.

So far as the Looe branch was concerned, the line was probably working at maximum capacity. In fine weather on summer Sundays at the height of the season, many trippers would visit Looe by train, and on the first down services of the day up to seven coaches would be required. On the return working in the afternoon, when the trippers would be brought back to catch the connecting main-line service to Plymouth, these long trains required banking from Coombe Junction to Liskeard. As there was no early passenger and goods duty on a Sunday, the second loco-motive at Moorswater would be steamed especially for this purpose. The expense of this, along with the overtime payments for the crew, was another example of the oper-ating expenses incurred by the railway in handling the incredible amounts of traffic being offered, expenses that were resulting in an increasing deficit in spite of the apparent heavy usage of the line. For, of course, although the line was heavily used during July and August, for the remainder of the year traffic was lighter and particularly sparse in the winter months. Five coaches was the norm on

these busy Sundays and the same number could occasion-ally be found on weekdays in the summer, spare coaches being held at Liskeard to strengthen trains when required. Two or three coaches were more than enough on the winter service.

At the time of writing, we are still able to trace former railway staff from the 1950s and so gain an impression of the everyday working of the line. On the locomotive side, there were three sets of enginemen at Moorswater to work the service. In the mid-1950s, they were drivers Bill Chapman, Jack Marshall and Stan Cole, and firemen were Keith Trembeth, Ron Bray and Pat Rickard. Only a few years previously, Albert Bray, along with Bill Hocking, had been firemen at Moorswater. Both of these men were ex-Liskeard and Looe Railway employees who, when the GWR had taken over working the line, had not been prepared to move away to gain promotion, so remained at Moorswater on the same grade throughout their working lives. Drivers Harry Menhennick and Jack Marshall had also been employees of the L & LR but, being younger and thus not settled, had moved elsewhere on the GWR system to gain promotion as drivers, although they had transferred back to Moorswater at their own request as soon as possible. Thus was created the anomaly of the firemen on the branch being older than their drivers, the reverse of the usual situation, although those former employees of the independent railway had largely retired by the mid-1950s. Driver Harry Menhennick retired during this period, at the age of 65, and was replaced by Bill Chapman who transferred to Moorswater from Tavistock.

Harry Menhennick had been the senior driver at Moorswater and liaised with the parent depot at St. Blazey on such matters as ordering stores and the like. Following his retirement, Jack Marshall became the senior driver.

Passenger guards were Stan Salter and Archie Screech whilst the goods guards were Alfie Hunt and Harry Buddle. Although the passenger guards were limited to the branch, the goods guards also worked on the main line. This duty involved relieving the guard of the 9.25 a.m. Tavistock Junction—Doublebois goods at Liskeard and working the train forward to its destination. The guard then stayed with the train on its return through to Tavistock Junction, east of Plymouth, returning to Liskeard 'on the cushions'. It was the practice for goods guards to work one week on, one week off this duty, alternating with the regular branch goods duty.

The day's working commenced with the early-turn fireman of the first passenger train booking on duty at Moorswater shed. All the crews lived in the vicinity of the shed and Keith Trembeth, whose recollections form the basis of these notes, would cycle up the path to Moorswater, passing beneath the viaduct, from his home at Lamellion. Although the engine was due off shed around 6.15 a.m., there was generally little for the fireman to do. Overnight the shedman/cleaner would have coaled the locomotive, directly from a coal wagon stabled at the back of the engine shed, cleaned the engine, built up the fire and raised steam. In fine weather the engine might even have been moved outside and the tanks filled with water. On arrival at about 5.10 a.m., the fireman made his way through the shed to the messroom at the back and brewed a pot of tea. When the driver arrived, he oiled the motion and axleboxes of the engine and did the routine checks of brake blocks and the like.

In the meantime the signalman at Liskeard Branch signal box had booked on at 6.10 a.m. and given the 'opening box' signal on the block instruments to the signalman at Coombe Junction who had booked on at the same time. When ready, amidst clouds of steam from the open cylinder drain cocks, the engine ran down to the shunting signal at Coombe Junction. Once the signal had cleared, the engine ran through the station and, picking up the single line token from the signalman at the window of his 'box, ran light to Liskeard.

On arrival in the Looe branch yard, the first job was to sort the wagons that had been left in the yard by the overnight main-line goods trains. These wagons had been detached from the main-line train and simply left at the entrance to the 'Looe' yard. Sorting often included taking wagons to the sidings, cattle dock and goods shed at the west end of Liskeard station, with the Liskeard branch signalman serving as shunter. He kept his shunter's pole in the porch at the top of the steps of his signal box. When the shunting was completed, the engine was coupled onto the coaches that were to form the first passenger train of the day. The signalman coupled the engine to the train, which

No. 4505 drifting down to Coombe Junction from Moorswater on 30th August 1954. *R. C. Riley*

The shunt signal beside Lamellion bridge that controlled access to Coombe Junction. *C. Gordon Watford*

was then drawn forward out of the yard and set back into the platform to await the arrival of the passengers. During the summer months, the first down train, the 7.15 a.m., would be well filled with hotel workers, waitresses, maids, etc., travelling to work in the hotels at Looe. This train was shown in the working timetable as a mixed train and would convey a few wagons if required.

Return from Looe was at 8.10 a.m. with arrival back at Liskeard scheduled for 8.41 a.m. The next working was from Liskeard at 8.55 a.m. with arrival at Looe timed at

9.24 a.m. At the same time the second Moorswater engine had come off shed at 9.30 a.m. and run light to Liskeard to pick up the second set of coaches which formed the 9.55 a.m. departure. After this train had made the cautious descent to Coombe Junction, it ran into the platform road, and by the time the engine had run round its coaches, the 9.45 a.m. ex-Looe had arrived at the Coombe Junction home signal. On those occasions when things went adrift and the train from Looe arrived at the Coombe Junction home signal before the train from Liskeard had arrived, it

No. 4565 with a morning departure from Liskeard on 1st July 1956.   *R. J. Sellick*

Left: Surrendering the tablet at Coombe Junction in July 1966. *Right:* Arriving at Coombe Junction on 22nd June 1956.

Author and Hugh Davies

Having placed the tail lamp on the lamp-iron at the rear of the train, guard Jim Richards is seen making his way along the platform at Coombe Junction while the engine moved towards the headshunt. *J. L. Rapson*

This view, looking back from the train on 11th August 1951, shows the engine moving onto the engine release crossover. *H. F. Wheeller*

Coombe Junction signal box at 5.45 p.m. on 4th July 1959. No. 4552 on the loop was on an unadvertised extra working from Liskeard which was waiting for the 5.17 p.m. departure from Looe which had just arrived in the charge of No. 4559.

Peter W. Gray

The engine backing onto the train on 18th August 1954.

H. C. Casserley

Fireman Keith Trembeth recoupling the engine to the train at Coombe Junction.

J. L. Rapson

A Looe-bound train waiting in the loop at Coombe Junction for an up train to arrive on 11th August 1951.   *H. F. Wheeller*

Two trains at Coombe Junction on the morning of 7th September 1959.   *R. J. Sellick*

This picture, taken at 9.5 a.m. at Coombe Junction on 2nd August 1958, shows No. 4585 in the platform with the 8.40 a.m. from Looe and the 8.45 a.m. from Liskeard leaving the loop. Once this train was clear, No. 4585 would run round its train before leaving on the final leg of its journey. The timings of this daily ritual varied over the years and it was also repeated when unadvertised extra trains were run.

Peter W. Gray

would be held at the signal. The train descending the steep gradient from Liskeard was always given priority to enter Coombe Junction platform and to perform the reversal shunting movements first.

With the run-round completed and the engine re-attached to the Looe end of the train, the 9.55 a.m. then drew forward back up the line towards Liskeard until it was clear of the junction. Once the signalman had reversed the points, the train then backed into the goods line and waited for the 9.45 a.m. ex-Looe to draw into the platform. With tokens duly exchanged and the road and signals set, the 9.55 a.m. was sent on its way to Looe, leaving the loop and goods line clear for the engine of the 9.45 a.m. to run round its train, and depart on the final part of its journey

to Liskeard where it arrived at 10.17 a.m. The second engine reached Looe at 10.26 a.m. and then worked the passenger service for the remainder of the day, making seven round trips in all, with the final arrival at Liskeard at 9.01 p.m.

In the meantime the engine of the 10.17 a.m. arrival at Liskeard very promptly stabled the coaches in the yard and set about assembling the morning goods train to Moorswater and Looe. According to the Working Timetable, the branch goods was due to leave the Looe branch yard at Liskeard at 12.10 a.m. − after the 11.57 a.m. passenger departure − but in practice, and strictly unofficially, the goods was usually sent down to Moorswater in advance of the passenger train. The reason for this divergence from the

No. 4552, with the Looe goods, shunting at Moorswater on 18th July 1960. *R. C. Riley*

Lunchtime at Moorswater. *M. E. J. Deane*

working timetable is that the crew took their meal break at Moorswater and an early departure from Liskeard meant a longer break. All the crews lived in the vicinity of Moorswater and when Harry Menhennick was on the goods turn, his wife would bring his lunch down to the yard. This was particularly important as he had a medical complaint which required a special diet. Keith Trembeth recalls that he would cycle down the path to Lamellion and enjoy the luxury of going home for lunch! In due course, with the shunting completed, the goods train left Moorswater yard for Looe, now following the timetable, in which departure

was shown as 1.00 p.m. with arrival at the terminus at 1.28 p.m.

Shunting at Looe then took a generous hour although movements had to cease whilst the passenger train arrived at 1.52 p.m. and drew into the yard for the engine to run round its train before departing again at 2.02 p.m. The goods departed from Looe at 2.30 p.m. and with a brief visit to Moorswater from 2.52 p.m. to 3.05 p.m., arrived at Liskeard at 3.20 p.m. After the wagons had been sorted and left for collection by passing main-line goods trains, the locomotive ran light back to Moorswater where the crew

Having completed its work at Moorswater, No. 4552 is seen here approaching Lamellion bridge and Coombe Junction with the branch goods train on 18th July 1960.　　　*R. C. Riley*

The arrival of the goods at Looe with No. 4552 on 18th July 1960.

R. C. Riley

While the goods train was at Looe, shunting operations had to cease whilst the passenger train came and went. This was the scene in
September 1961.

G. Tilt

might book off duty. Occasionally it was necessary for the 'Looe goods' engine and brake van to run down the main line to the next station at Menheniot to collect loaded ballast wagons from Clicker Tor Quarry. Running when required, the engine brought the wagons back to Liskeard where they were stabled in the down side 'engine shed' sidings or in the up sidings in the Looe branch yard, depending on where they were ultimately destined. Ballast wagons were generally worked forward by passing overnight goods trains.

On arrival back at Moorswater in the late afternoon, the early-turn engine would be secured in the shed and left for the overnight shedman, 'Brit' Arthur Martin, to deal with when he booked on at 10.0 p.m. During the latter part of the duty, the fireman would allow the fire to die down so that there was little left when the engine arrived at Moorswater. As the engine was left in light steam, the shed doors were closed and locked to prevent any unauthorised tampering. In due course, the late-turn engine would also return and be left for the shedman.

All the crews considered that they were fortunate to have the services of the shedman as, at the beginning of their shift, there was little for them to do, most of the preparation work having already been done for them. Generally, the work on the branch was pleasant and easy although, when working passenger trains, the firemen found coupling and uncoupling the engine at each end of every round trip and during the reversal at Coombe Junction to be something of a chore.

The service was a little different on summer Saturdays with the first departure at 5.50 a.m. from Liskeard and the correspondingly earlier starts for all concerned. This early train would often carry numbers of arriving holidaymakers who had travelled down by overnight trains from their homes 'up-country'. On Friday and Saturday evenings an extra 'fish and chip' train was run. This arrived back at Liskeard at 10.21 p.m. and meant a later finish for the staff.

As already related, on summer Sundays, it was often necessary to bank the early evening up train between

No. 5519 with the branch goods brake van at Moorswater.   *D. Laurence*

No. 4552 waiting at the shunt signal beside Lamellion bridge on 6th June 1956, perhaps prior to banking a train to Liskeard.

J. H. G. Coltas

Coombe Junction and Liskeard. On such occasions the second locomotive at Moorswater would be specially steamed for the purpose, the preparation work being done by the fireman, as the shedman took his day off on a Sunday. When the up passenger train was due to arrive at Coombe Junction, the second engine would run quietly down to the shunting signal by Lamellion bridge where it would wait. On arrival from Looe, the train engine would remain coupled to the train in the platform and become the assisting engine for the climb from Coombe Junction to Liskeard. Once the shunting signal had cleared, the second engine would run through the goods line and set back onto the train, thus becoming the train engine. The driver of what was now the train engine would signal that he was ready by giving two 'crows' on the whistle, which would be acknowledged by the driver of the assisting engine, after which the train would depart for Liskeard. As the assisting engine passed the signal box, the fireman would collect the token from the signalman.

Journey time from Coombe Junction to Liskeard was only eight minutes and, providing it had a good clean hot fire, this brief burst of activity for the second engine could be achieved with only two or three shovelfuls of coal being added on the ascent. After the final 1 in 60 gradient into Liskeard station, the banker would ease off and allow the train engine to draw the train into the platform at the regulation 5 mph. Once the fireman had surrendered the token to the Liskeard branch signalman, the banking engine would be detached from the train and be taken into the yard to shunt the coaching stock. Once released from the train, the second locomotive would run light engine to Moorswater for disposal and stabling.

An important constituent of the goods turn was the removal of loaded china clay wagons from the dries at

Liskeard on 23rd June 1959 with No. 4552 on the train and No. 5539 in the siding.   *Author's collection*

No. 4585 returning to Liskeard with the empty coaching stock of a down extra train near Terras level crossing on 11th July 1959.

Peter W. Gray

Moorswater. These wagons were taken to Liskeard and left at the down side 'engine shed' sidings to be worked forward by down main-line goods trains. The number of loaded wagons that could be worked up the gradient to Liskeard by a single locomotive was strictly limited by a notice in the Appendix to the Working Timetable. Twelve wagons of general merchandise (Class 2) or nine wagons of minerals (Class 1) was the maximum permitted load and, as the other Moorswater locomotive was working the passenger service, there was no spare engine available to assist. Although china clay was labelled as a Class 2 traffic, i.e. general merchandise, it was loaded and worked as Class 1 traffic, i.e. minerals, and therefore nine loaded clay wagons was the maximum permitted load.

When a ship was loading at Fowey, it was sometimes necessary to make two or three journeys between Moorswater and Liskeard to clear the loaded wagons and assemble them into a train in the main-line sidings at Liskeard. When there was such an urgent requirement at Fowey, overtime payments were made to the Moorswater crew to enable the work to be done quickly. In addition, a St. Blazey engine, sometimes a '42XX' 2—8—0T, would come up to Liskeard specially to collect the loaded wagons. Less urgently required consignments were taken forward to Fowey or Par by passing goods trains.

Until 1956, apart from the china clay traffic from Moorswater, the only other significant flow of goods traffic was coal to the gasworks at Looe, and it was when the gasworks closed during this period that serious economic questions were being addressed at the highest levels of BR management. In 1955, British Railways announced a £1,240 million Modernization Plan which, amongst other aims, proposed the elimination of steam traction on all routes west of Newton Abbot by 1959. When the future of the Liskeard and Looe line was examined, it was considered to be an unremunerative branch. Although the postwar tourism boom meant that the line was extremely busy during the summer months, as already explained, during the winter, trains on the line were lightly loaded. A survey conducted from October 1954 to May 1955 reveals that there were only 72 local passengers each weekday and there were daily averages of only 121 tickets issued. A factor in the decline of traffic was that the railway was suffering from unrestricted competition from local bus operators, the

No. 4559 leaving Coombe Junction for Liskeard with loaded china clay wagons from Moorswater dries on 18th August 1959. *P. Hay*

No. 4565 climbing from Coombe Junction with the 8.40 a.m. from Looe on 15th August 1959.

Peter W. Gray

Such was the demand for the lunchtime train to Looe on 7th August 1961 that extra coaches had to be added. This view shows the expectant throng on the platform at Liskeard waiting for the additional coaches to be added to the three already standing at the platform.
P. Barnfield

1952 Transport Act having swept away any notion of an integrated bus/rail service. Indeed, the conclusion of the survey mentioned that, outside the summer peak, the branch trains 'load lightly — rarely beyond the capacity of a double-deck bus'.

By the latter part of the 1950s, the postwar holiday boom reached its peak and the railway was seriously challenged by road traffic, both from buses and by the private motorist, as the number of cars was increasing dramatically as a result of the newly-found affluence. A further factor in the decline of traffic was the two-week ASLEF strike in 1955, which caused the loss of substantial amounts of freight traffic to the roads, much of which never returned to the railway.

In the event, the proposal to eliminate steam by 1959 was over-optimistic. However, the writing was clearly on the wall for many West Country branch lines. The scheme had envisaged the closure of the majority of such lines, but by 1959, although it had been found that the Liskeard and Looe branch was an 'unremunerative railway passenger service', it was considered that the service would have to be retained on a permanent basis but that economies in working would have to be found. Use of diesel multiple units was proposed and a test run was made so that an estimate of savings could be calculated.

On Tuesday, 6th October 1959, a two-car high-density diesel set arrived at Liskeard from Belmont sidings, Plymouth, having worked down from Bristol the previous day. Departing Liskeard at 10.40 a.m., the very first diesel train arrived at Looe at 11.35 a.m. in the charge of the Plymouth, Laira tutor driver. After a stop-over at Looe, during which time the regular service train came and went, the diesel unit left at 1.05 p.m., arriving back at Liskeard at 1.50 p.m. At 2.10 p.m. the train left again for Plymouth, returning to Bristol on Wednesday, 7th October. The trial run was evidently a success, but it was to be almost two years before steam was removed from the Looe branch, due almost certainly to delays in delivery of new trains. The introduction of diesel multiple units brought a revision in the passenger timetable to allow one unit to operate the service and avoid the need to cross passenger trains at Coombe Junction.

In due course plans were made and the summer of 1961 was the last in which steam locomotives worked on the Liskeard and Looe branch. The fateful day was Sunday, 10th September — the last day of the summer service — and the occasion was recognized locally, being reported by *The Cornish Times* in its edition of 15th September 1961:

DIESEL FOR THE 'LOOE EXPRESS'
A strange silence prevailed over the Looe branch line on Monday morning. Cattle and sheep in adjacent fields were decidedly puzzled, and the birds kept an amazed silence as the 7.5 a.m. 'Looe Express' rolled by.

Gone was the tough little engine, billowing clouds of smoke and steam over the hillsides, gone, too, were the dirty, dusty coaches which it used to pull. In its place was a rather smart looking light and airy diesel car, for the steam era had made its exit from the branch line on Sunday evening.

FUNERAL RITES
As is customary on such occasions, the train was accorded the full funeral rites. A contingent of the Liskeard Drama Group, in heavy mourning, headed a procession of well-wishers and sightseers down the branch line platform at Liskeard station, to pay their last respects.

Mrs. R. R. B. Kitson, of Morval, decorated the spars and buffers on the front of the engine with flowers given by Liskeard people, and Mr. Harvey Lister, keeping a stiff upper lip, solemnly placed an evergreen wreath around the old engine's funnel. The party then made the trip to Looe.

A large placard, carrying the words 'Farewell to steam' informed anyone who did not already know, what all the fuss was about, as the mourners waited silently on the Looe platform for the engine to change ends for its last trip on the branch.

Then, at a signal from the guard, Mr. Cyril Willis, the train pulled out in a shower of smoke and smuts, with both ordinary and emergency whistles at full blast. Crowds of people on the platform cheered and waved, and fog signal detonators, exploding on the line generally added importance to the occasion.

British Railways had no time for sentimentalities. To them it was just another event. Liskeard's stationmaster (Mr. Tom Pickard) watched the performance from a discreet distance. The train driver, 60-years-old Mr. Stanley Cole, who has been going backwards and forwards on the line for the past 16 years, had no regrets about leaving the steam age, in fact, he welcomed the change.

"Diesels are cleaner and more convenient than steam", he said. "You can't stop progress."

A little of the gilt was knocked off the occasion when a 'Cornish Times' reporter asked Mr. Cole if he had any pet name for the 'old faithful'.

"I wouldn't like to tell you what I do call it sometimes", he replied. Fireman Pat Rickard had similar views.

The 30-years-old steam engine will not be pensioned off entirely. It will be going to another branch line in Cornwall for further sterling service.

The new Looe diesel is part of a regional dieselisation scheme to try to save some of the branch lines from closing, by making economies in running costs.

Type 2 diesel hydraulic No. D6320 approaching Coombe Junction with china clay wagons from Moorswater on 5th July 1963.

R. C. Riley

The first train worked by a diesel multiple unit was the 7.5 a.m. Liskeard to Looe service on Monday 11th September — the start of the winter timetable. Goods services, too, were henceforth worked by diesel locomotives of the Type 2 Bo-Bo diesel hydraulic 'D63XX' class, a test run having been made on 4th March 1959. A recast service of eight return trips was provided by the new diesel trains, with an extra late service running on Saturday evenings. Weekday services were increased to nine return trips in 1965 whilst on summer Saturdays ten or eleven trains were run.

It was soon found that diesel working was not reducing operating costs sufficiently and a further threat to the future of the line came in March 1963 when the fateful 'Reshaping of British Railways' — better known as the 'Beeching Report' — was published. By 1961 one in nine people in Britain owned a motor car; in 1938 ownership had been less than two million private cars and this had grown to six million by 1961. Even local bus services were suffering and, with improvement to roads and an increasing requirement for door-to-door traffic, lorries were carrying more and more traffic that traditionally had been the preserve of the railways. The operating deficit had gone through the roof and it had been realized that, by 1960, only ten per cent of travellers were going by train. A comprehensive railway network was therefore thought to be unnecessary and, in the 'Beeching Report', the Looe branch, losing £1,037 per annum, was listed for closure. Indeed, in 1965 even more drastic cuts for Cornwall were proposed when the demise of the entire railway network west of Plymouth was considered. The opening of the Tamar road bridge in 1962 had made its effect on railway traffic whilst

there were doubts about the long-term future of Brunel's Royal Albert Bridge at Saltash.

Goods services on the Looe branch were withdrawn on 4th November 1963 with the exception of china clay traffic from Moorswater to Liskeard. Complete closure of the line was proposed in 1966, the fateful day was to have been 5th October, when passenger trains would have ceased. Although the usual objections were heard at an enquiry, closure was scheduled by British Railways, yet in the event the line was reprieved. The Labour Government's Minister of Transport, Mrs. Barbara Castle, refused to sanction the closure due to the difficulties in providing an alternative bus service through the narrow lanes, particularly in the summer months.

Further economies were made when Looe station was destaffed from Monday, 30th September 1968. Tickets were henceforth purchased from the conductor/guard on the trains, and other functions were transferred to Liskeard station. From 1969 the line received subsidies from the Ministry of Transport in the form of a grant equal to the operating deficit.

Additional economies came in 1970 when the level crossing at Terras was destaffed, whilst in 1981 Coombe Junction signal box was closed, the train crews henceforth working the junction themselves. And there matters remain until the present, with the line continuing to serve the area much as it has since passenger services commenced in 1879. Who can tell what the future holds, for, with recent privatization of the railway system, there are a new set of uncertainties, and 'market forces' may yet hold a threat for the Liskeard and Looe branch.

LOCOMOTIVES AND ROLLING STOCK

Caradon with a special train for a Sunday school outing at Polwrath on the L & C Line in the early 1900s. *L & GRP*

AT the turn of the 20th century, passenger services between Moorswater and Looe remained the responsibility of the impecunious Liskeard and Caradon Company which was still using the same three engines that had been provided following the introduction of locomotive power and the opening of the line to Looe. The oldest of the locomotives in service was *Caradon*, an 0—6—0ST built by Gilkes, Wilson & Co. of Middlesborough in 1862. With 4ft diameter driving wheels and a coupled wheelbase of approximately 6ft 4in x 5ft 2in, the outside cylinders drove onto the middle set of driving wheels which were flangeless. The locomotive is believed to have received a new firebox, and possibly a boiler also, from the Avonside Engine Co. in 1878, and is reported to have been rebuilt in 1899, thus making her in good condition at the turn of the century. Indeed, at this time she was providing the backbone of the service, and there was concern that if she broke down, the company would be in serious difficulty as the other two engines were in poor condition.

In 1902 a report on the company's locomotives and rolling stock included the following extract, which gives an impression of the work necessary at Moorswater to keep the motive power in working order:

'The "Caradon" was the only engine undergoing repair and I was able to examine the interior of the firebox just as it came in. Nothing had been done to it and the firebox stays, plates, tube ends presented a most favourable appearance considering the hard living they are subjected to on the gradients. The wheel tyre flanges are worn and will be turned up and the driving set are away at Newton Abbot to be fitted with a new crankpin, the original having been lately broken on the road. The left-hand cylinder cover was off having been broken together with the

crosshead, a new one has been made and the other parts repaired.'

By 1906, however, the locomotive was reported to be in need of constant attention as the frame was split and she was withdrawn in 1907 and presumably broken up at Moorswater. As mentioned elsewhere, her firebox wrapper was retained and, fitted with wooden doors, was mounted over a fast-flowing stream to provide a very primitive lavatory· for staff at the shed. Following the closure of Moorswater shed, the firebox was left in situ and was certainly still there in 1966 when the writer visited the site. It has subsequently been preserved and is presently to be found at the former Bodmin General station but not in use as a lavatory!

Cheesewring was the second locomotive obtained by the L & CR from Gilkes, Wilson & Co. in 1864. With a shorter wheelbase of 4ft 4in x 4ft 4in and with driving wheels of 4ft diameter, she was of the 'long boiler' type with the firebox behind the rear driving axle.

The outside cylinders drove to the trailing wheels whilst the centre driving wheels were again flangeless. By 1885 it is recorded as the only fit engine on the railway, and was rebuilt in 1890 with a boiler having a dome on the middle ring and a tank of 700 gallons capacity over the barrel only. By 1906 the repairs necessary to the engine were beyond the ability of the staff at Moorswater to undertake and quotes were obtained from outside contractors, including Pecketts of Bristol. Prices quoted were too high, and in 1907 *Cheesewring* was despatched to the GWR works at Swindon where she received a heavy general overhaul.

Cheesewring at rest inside Old Oak Common roundhouse in 1919, positively dwarfed by a GWR 4—4—2 'County' tank.   *L & GRP*

When the Great Western took over responsibility for working the line in 1909, *Cheesewring* received the GWR number 1311, the new numberplates being attached to the bunker sidesheets, but otherwise her appearance did not change. *Cheesewring* remained at Moorswater until February 1917, by which time the Caradon line had closed, and it is thought probable that from 1914 onwards she was the only locomotive which ventured northwards from Moorswater. Certainly the light nature of the track would have prevented the use of any heavier locomotives.

After four months in the Bristol area, and an even shorter spell at Severn Tunnel Junction, *Cheesewring* was sent to the London area where she spent the remainder of her existence. Allocated to the premier GWR shed at Old Oak Common, her antique appearance must have made a considerable contrast to the standard GWR classes that she shared the shed with, and doubtless she did not prove too attractive to the engine crews who had to work her. She was employed in shunting at a munitions factory at Greenford and continued this job of national importance until August 1919 when she was withdrawn from service.

Third of the old Liskeard and Caradon Railway engines in use at the turn of the century was *Kilmar*. Built in 1869 by Hopkins, Gilkes and Co. — successors to Gilkes, Wilson and Co. — it is believed to have been built to the same

dimensions as *Cheesewring*. *Kilmar* broke down in 1885 and was apparently out of use until 1887, when a new boiler was obtained from Vulcan Foundry of Newton-le-Willows, Lancashire. In 1902 *Kilmar* was sent to Avonside Engine Co. at Bristol for major repairs, and it is thought that the large cab was fitted at this time. She was noted as requiring constant attention by 1906 and in 1908 was despatched to Swindon works where she received heavy repairs. When the GWR took over working the line, *Kilmar* received the number 1312 and she remained in her old haunts, mostly allocated to Moorswater but also spending periods working from the engine shed at Looe. She was withdrawn from service in May 1914 having arrived at Swindon works for disposal on 23rd April.

With the imminent opening of the new connecting line to Liskeard, the directors of the Liskeard and Looe Railway set about providing a new locomotive to work the service. It was intended that the existing locomotives should work the old line to Caradon and that the new engine would work the passenger service between Looe and Liskeard. It was envisaged that a modern version of the old L & C locomotives would suffice but with larger cylinders to cope with the gradients. Quotes were obtained from Pecketts of Bristol, but in the event the order went to Robert Stephenson & Co. of Newcastle.

Looe as London & India Docks Co. No. 11. *Collection P. Q. Treloar*

The quote for the new locomotive was received from the makers on 7th June 1900 and stated that the 'cost of the locomotive would be £1,995 delivered to Liskeard within five months from receipt of order'. Rather prophetically, the quote also offered the information that 'we have just sent three similar engines to London & India Docks Joint Committee where they are giving every satisfaction'. Acknowledgement of receipt of the order in August 1900 from the builders gave the specification for the new engine. It was to be a 'saddle tank locomotive with outside cylinders 16in diameter x 20in stroke, six cast steel wheels 3ft 6in diameter and coupled, tyres of steel, axles of wrot-iron, boiler of Siemens—Martin mild steel, copper firebox, brass tubes, 2 x No. 7 injectors, screw brake applied to front sides of all the wheels, engine also fitted with auto-matic vaccum brake, tank to contain 700 gallons of water'. The engine had the maker's number 3050 and was to carry the name *Looe*.

Looe was delivered in April 1901 in time for the opening of the new line and arrived in company with an NER wagon loaded with a case containing the side rods, tools, etc, the ensemble having travelled from Newcastle via Manchester, Warrington and then over the GW and LNW joint line. Robert Stephenson sent a fitter, Septimus Cotton, to accompany the engine and prepare it for service. In August 1901 Cotton was persuaded to stay on at Moorswater as Locomotive Superintendent and Foreman of repairs shops. One can imagine the impact of his Geordie accent on the local Cornish vernacular!

Unfortunately, *Looe* was not a great success. She worked the first passenger train on the new line, but very soon developed a reputation for running out of steam on the climb up to Liskeard. In addition, she became derailed on her first visit to Looe and suffered the same misfortune

at Coombe Junction on 22nd May 1901. Due to the light nature and poor condition of the track between Coombe Junction and Looe, it was soon decided that the new engine was too heavy for satisfactory operation of the passenger service. As an interim measure, it was proposed that the service would be maintained with the old L & C engines, of which *Caradon* was the only one fully serviceable, and that *Looe* should be disposed of and another, more suitable, locomotive obtained.

Negotiàtions were opened with the London & India Docks Co. and in due course they offered to purchase *Looe* for £1,400. She left Liskeard on 14th April 1902 and as she was to travel 'dead', i.e. not in steam, the side rods were taken down to avoid damage to the cylinders whilst in transit. She worked at the Royal Victoria Dock, London, as that company's No. 11, and gave every satisfaction to her new owners. In due course, she passed into the ownership of the Port of London Authority — also carrying their number 11 — and was scrapped in December 1950, outliving her replacement by just over two years.

To cover the interim period until a new locomotive could be obtained, an engine was hired from the GWR. As soon as the decision for the disposal of *Looe* had been made, quotes were obtained for its replacement. The specif-ication issued to several builders included the following requirements: 'side tank, bunker at back, inside cylinder 15in diameter x 22in stroke, 4ft diameter driving wheels, four wheel coupled with leading bogie or radial boxes on leading wheels, weight not to exceed 30 tons, wheels to be fitted with water jets, cab on all parts to clear overline bridge 11ft 6in, required to draw load of 90 tons up an incline of 1 in 40, 1½ miles long, be able to take curve of 8 chain radius'. Thus were learned the lessons of the unhappy experience with *Looe*! Robert Stephenson & Co. quoted

£1,800 for this 2—4—0 side tank whilst Avonsides of Bristol were also considered, given their reputation for cheapness and quality of locomotives. In the event, the order went to Andrew Barclay & Co. of Kilmarnock, who quoted a price of £1,570, delivered to Liskeard GWR, 18 to 20 weeks from receipt of order.

The new 2—4—0T was named *Lady Margaret* after Captain Spicer's wife — Spicer had largely financed the construction of the new line as well as the purchase of the new engine and its predecessor *Looe*. She was built largely to the specification with a wheelbase of 6ft x 7ft, leading wheels 2ft 7½in, driving wheels 4ft diameter, cylinders 14½in x 22in and weighed 28 tons. In November 1902 it

was reported that 'the loco is very satisfactory' and it was further stated that 'it is very gratifying to see that the loco can make up steam on the bank and it proves that she is the right type for the job'. *Lady Margaret* required little attention during the period of ownership by the Liskeard and Looe Railway and the company at last had a modern, reliable locomotive to work the passenger service.

In 1909 the engine received the GWR number 1308, the brass plates being affixed to the bunker sides. She remained working on the line, spending alternate periods of several months at Moorswater and Looe. Works visits when necessary were made to the GWR factory at Newton Abbot with a visit, from March to August 1911, to Swindon for more

Lady Margaret shunting at Swindon on 6th July 1921 as GWR No. 1308. *L & GRP*

An immaculate No. 13 at Looe in 1909 with fireman Bill Hocking on the footplate. *L & GRP*

No. 13 at Looe on 21st
October 1921.
P. J. T. Reed

thorough attention. By 1920 *Lady Margaret* was spending some time at Plymouth but for much of the summer of that year she was stationed at Moorswater as usual. She left Moorswater for Plymouth for the last time in November 1920, and in 1921 was at Swindon where she was often to be seen shunting around the works yards. Almost immediately after the grouping in 1923, *Lady Margaret* was sent to Oswestry to enable the smaller, former Cambrian Railways engines to be released for repair. She stayed in Wales for the remainder of her existence except for a brief spell following rebuilding with a new boiler in 1929, when she was allocated to Exeter to work on the Culm Valley line from Tiverton Junction to Hemyock. In Mid Wales her principal duty was to work the former Tanat Valley Light Railway where she seems to have been as successful as she was on the Liskeard and Looe line for she remained there until May 1948 when she was withdrawn.

The locomotive hired from the GWR in 1901 was a 4—4—0 saddle tank No. 13, but it is interesting to note that an approach was also considered to Holbrook's former employers, the Great Eastern Railway. No. 13 was a locomotive with an interesting history. Built as a 2—4—2T in 1886, instead of the usual side tanks, it had tanks at the back and between the frames. She is known to have worked on the Abingdon branch in Oxfordshire and had already spent some time in Cornwall where she had been employed on the St. Ives branch. In 1897 No. 13 was rebuilt into a 4—4—0 saddle tank and in 1901 received a new boiler with an extended smokebox. In this form she spent a short period on the Highworth branch before being sent on hire to the Liskeard and Looe Railway.

She remained on the line for much of the next twenty years, initially for periods of hire to the L & LR, and she remained there from 1909 onwards after the GWR had taken over working the line. With her short, fixed wheelbase and flexible four-wheeled bogie, No. 13 must have been a very suitable engine for the Looe line with the

lightly laid and poorly maintained track. From January to September 1906, however, No. 13 was at Brixham, working on the short branch from Churston, but by 1907 she was back at Moorswater. The terms for the hire of No. 13 were, in 1907, a charge of two shillings per hour for the whole time the engine was in steam, with a minimum charge of £1 for any one working day. The L & LR Co. were to provide workmen, fuel and stores, and were to pay for the whole time occupied by the engine in going to and returning from the depot.

From 1909 No. 13 was stationed more or less permanently on the line, alternating with No. 1308 *Lady Margaret* between Moorswater and Looe. In 1919 No. 13 began spending more time at Plymouth, at the old Millbay shed and could often be seen shunting carriage stock at North Road station. She left Moorswater for the last time in May 1922 and was sent to Swindon as a works shunter, eventually being withdrawn from service in May 1926.

Examination of the GWR locomotive allocation registers reveal that, in the period after 1909 when the GWR became responsible for working the line, a number of main-line engines were seemingly allocated to Moorswater shed. This may well be as a result of the reduction in status of the former Cornwall Railway engine shed at Liskeard as no allocation is recorded there after October 1912. In 1911 and 1912 'Metropolitan' class 2—4—0T No. 1457 is shown as allocated to Moorswater and likewise in 1920. Double-framed 0—6—0 saddle tank No. 1562, of the '1076' class, was there for a short period but neither was permitted to run down the line to Looe.

Smaller GWR classes were to be found at Moorswater from 1911 to assist the 'native' engines. The small, outside cylinder saddle tanks of the '1361' class, normally employed at St. Blazey for working the Goonbarrow branch, were employed intermittently, along with their predecessors, the ex Cornwall Minerals Railway 0—6—0 saddle tanks (No. 1395 was at Moorswater in 1917, for

'2021' class No. 2118
in the yard at Looe
c.1924.
Author's collection

example) whilst in 1918 an observer noted that the line was worked by 4—4—0ST No. 13 on the passenger service and '1361' class 0—6—0ST No. 1361 on the goods service.

In 1919 '850' class 0—6—0ST No. 1956 arrived at Moorswater from Plymouth Millbay shed, to supplement the regular engines Nos. 13 and 1308, which were spending more time away at Plymouth. Increasingly this class of Wolverhampton tank engines was used to work the service and, following the departure for Swindon of No. 13 in 1922, were solely used on the line. Between 1921 and 1925 the following examples were allocated to Moorswater shed to work the branch, Nos. 1940, 1941, 1973, 1985, 1992, 2020, being joined in 1924 by '2021' class 0—6—0PT Nos. 2062 and 2148. As is always the case though, other examples of the class worked on the line from time to time — '2021' class No. 2118, for example, was photographed at Looe but was undoubtedly a substitute, for she was normally employed on the Bodmin Road—Bodmin branch. It should be noted that Nos. 1973, 2020, 2062 and 2148 had already been fitted with pannier tanks before they worked on the Liskeard and Looe line.

Before going on to consider the more modern locomotive power, it would be as well to go back to the turn of the 20th century and examine the coaching stock in use on the line. As with the locomotives, the original coaching stock of 1879/80 was still in use by the L & CR and by 1900 was decidedly antiquated in appearance. Three coaches and a passenger brake van had been constructed by the Metropolitan Railway Carriage and Wagon Co. Ltd. at their Saltley works. They were oil lit and had particularly narrow bodies. The vehicles were delivered from Saltley to Plymouth on their own wheels, presumably using the mixed gauge route via Lydford and Tavistock to reach Plymouth,

whereupon they were loaded onto broad-gauge wagons for delivery to Liskeard. Transferring the vehicles from the GWR yard to the Liskeard and Caradon Railway yard at Moorswater must have been an interesting exercise!

In 1896 the coaches had been fitted with continuous vacuum brakes as a result of a Board of Trade directive and, incredibly, they survived to be taken over by the GWR in 1909 whereupon they were immediately scrapped.

New vehicles were ordered in 1901 to work the passenger service when the new extension to Liskeard was opened. Three bogie vehicles, with end doors and balconies, were built by Hurst Nelson & Co. of Motherwell, and like the locomotive *Looe*, ordered at the same time, were not a success. It is possible that they were not built sufficiently strong enough to work on the rough track of the old route to Looe and it is recorded that they had been sold by 1904. However, in 1906 all three vehicles remained on the line, being in store at Moorswater, and two were destroyed on 15th June by the runaway train which ran down from Liskeard. One vehicle and the remains of the other two were still on the line in 1909 and were quickly disposed of by the GWR.

By November 1903 the Liskeard and Looe Railway were considering the purchase of redundant locomotive-hauled, four-wheel coaches from the recently electrified Mersey Railway. Three coaches were delivered to the railway in January 1904 and in due course a total of thirteen were purchased. They were four-wheeled, vacuum-braked, gas-lit and were close-coupled, a relic of their service on the Mersey Railway. All had been built by the Ashbury Railway Carriage and Wagon Co., Openshaw, Manchester from 1885 to 1888. The acquisition of these vehicles, along with the purchase of the 2—4—0T *Lady Margaret*, at last provided the company with satisfactory stock with which to operate the passenger service, and they continued in use until 1909 when the GWR's working arrangement came into force.

It was a train of six of the ex Mersey Railway four-wheelers which formed the runaway train on 15th June 1906, but remarkably only one vehicle was destroyed in the smash, the others being only slightly damaged. Thus it was that twelve coaches were handed over to the GWR. It is not known for how long they continued in use on the Liskeard and Looe line but they were renumbered into GWR stock in August 1909. However, a photograph dated 1909 shows 4—4—0ST No. 13 at Causeland with a passenger train comprising GWR four-wheeled coaches, so the ex Mersey coaches may have left the area soon after the GWR working arrangement commenced. Six of the Mersey coaches were scrapped in September 1910 but the remaining six were transferred to the stock of the Rhondda and Swansea Bay Railway, for the running of which the GWR was responsible. In 1912 they returned to the GWR fold and were scrapped in 1913.

No. 13 with ex-Mersey Railway coaches at Looe in the 1900s.
Lens of Sutton

'850' class 0—6—0PT No. 1973 shunting at Looe.   *A. G. Ellis*

This line-up at St. Blazey on 5th August 1922 shows three classes of engine associated with the Looe branch in the 1920s. '1361' class No. 1364 (right) was on the line in 1912 and again in 1920, ex-Cornwall Minerals Railway No. 1398 (centre) was allocated to Looe in 1922, whilst the '45XX' class first appeared at Moorswater in 1926.   *Collection R. S. Carpenter*

'44XX' No. 4405 shunting fish vans on Looe Quay in 1927.   *Author's collection*

The coaches provided to work the line by the GWR were four- and six-wheelers of a type used on similar lines throughout the system. Constructed during the 1880s and 1890s, they were very similar to the former Mersey Railway coaches that they replaced, being gas-lit and built to similar dimensions, but of course were 'standard' GWR vehicles. In 1911 the Plymouth Division Carriage Working Programme specified that the branch train was to consist of the following vehicles: Brake Third, Third, Composite, Brake Third. Similar vehicles and formations remained in use until around 1930, the 1929 carriage programme specifying two sets of these coaches to work the service. By then, however, they would have looked rather old-fashioned and have presented a poor image of the company to the public.

When, in November 1924, '44XX' 2−6−2T No. 4400 was transferred to Moorswater, it started an association with the type that was to continue to the end of steam traction on the branch. This small class of eleven, built as a scaled-down version of the 'standard' Churchward designs, had been introduced in 1904-6 and were an instant success. They revolutionised the working of branch lines in the West Country, and St. Blazey was one of the first sheds to receive them, several being sent there new in 1906. So successful were they that it was soon decided to construct more of the type, but the coupled wheel diameter was increased, from 4ft 1½in to 4ft 7½in, thus giving the later engines an increased turn of speed. Originally numbered in the 2161-90 series, in 1912 they were renumbered in the '45XX' series and examples of these, too, were sent new to St. Blazey. Here they were principally employed on the services from Newquay to Par and Fowey and it was not until the 1920s that they appeared on the Liskeard and

Looe line, probably as a result of further examples of the type being built in 1924. Both the '44XX' and '45XX' class were always highly regarded by the enginemen that worked them — one ex St. Blazey fireman swears that they 'would steam on a flare lamp' — and they remained fully masters of their work until the diesels arrived.

At first No. 4400 shared the service with the 0–6–0 saddle and pannier tanks, but in February 1925 she was joined by No. 4410. The '2021' class No. 2148 left Moorswater in March 1925 and from that time on the 2–6–2Ts had sole charge of the branch services. No. 4406 also worked from Moorswater in 1925 whilst the first '45XX', No. 4523, arrived in June 1926. Further examples of the '45XX' were built from 1927 to 1929 and had larger tanks with increased water capacity. A hundred examples of these later 2–6–2Ts were built, numbered from 4575 to 5574, and the first example of the type, No. 4578, arrived at Moorswater late in 1927. Henceforth the 2–6–2Ts worked without exception, the allocation changing intermittently over the years as individual engines were called for works attention and were replaced by others. By the mid 1920s Moorswater was a sub-shed of St. Blazey and whilst some routine maintenance was undertaken by the enginemen, such as brake adjustments, locomotives returned to the parent depot fortnightly for boiler washouts, etc. Moorswater engines tended to be well looked after by the shedman and enginemen, and as far as possible St. Blazey

tried to return the same locomotives from regular maintenance.

Details of the locomotives allocated to Moorswater during the GWR period from 1923 until 1948 are given in the accompanying table, but it should be remembered that only two engines were at Moorswater at any one time. During the BR period, allocations at Moorswater were not specified, so any of the '45XX' 2–6–2Ts at St. Blazey could be expected to have been found on the line. During the earlier BR period, as a general rule, the earlier '45XX' with flat-topped tanks were employed on the shorter branches, such as Liskeard to Looe and Bodmin Road to Bodmin, whilst the '4575' series with larger tanks were used on the longer runs to Newquay. Latterly, the '4575' series predominated at Moorswater and it was one of this type which worked the last steam-powered train to Looe.

Although the last permanent allocation of a '44XX' to Moorswater was in 1946 (No. 4407), a driver recalls that one of them was working on the line in the early 1950s as a temporary replacement for the regular '45XX'. He particularly recalled that 'she ran like a sewing machine unlike the regular engine', but further details are not known.

In 1953 a number of the '4575' class were equipped with apparatus to work auto-trains in the Cardiff Valleys area of South Wales in conjunction with the introduction of a regular interval passenger timetable. Fifteen of the class were so fitted and, when the Cardiff Valleys service

'45XX' No. 4515 on Looe Quay in 1928. *D. B. Hart*

ENGINE ALLOCATIONS TO MOORSWATER 1923-1948

Year	Number	Class	Year	Number	Class	Year	Number	Class	Year	Number	Class
1923	1220	850 class	1931	4400	44XX class	1938	4410	44XX class	1946	4407	44XX class
	1941	850 class		4401	44XX class		4502	45XX class		4503	45XX class
	1973	850 class		4406	44XX class		4528	45XX class		4505	45XX class
	1985	850 class		4407	44XX class		4531	45XX class		4529	45XX class
	1992	850 class		4502	45XX class		4534	45XX class		4552	45XX class
	2020	850 class		4531	45XX class		4538	45XX class		4559	45XX class
				4542	45XX class		4545	45XX class		4565	45XX class
1924	1941	850 class		4544	45XX class					4568	45XX class
	1973	850 class		4548	45XX class	1939	4410	44XX class		4570	45XX class
	1992	850 class		4553	45XX class		4502	45XX class		4598	4575 class
	2020	850 class		4556	45XX class		4528	45XX class		5502	4575 class
	2062	2021 class		4558	45XX class		4531	45XX class		5519	4575 class
	2148	2021 class		4576	4575 class		4542	45XX class		5531	4575 class
	4400	44XX class		5502	4575 class		4598	4575 class			
	4405	44XX class					5519	4575 class	1947	4503	45XX class
			1932	4401	44XX class		5531	4575 class		4505	45XX class
1925	1941	850 class		4406	44XX class					4529	45XX class
	2148	2021 class		4531	45XX class	1940	4531	45XX class		4552	45XX class
	4400	44XX class		4538	45XX class		4583	4575 class		4559	45XX class
	4406	44XX class		4542	45XX class		5519	4575 class		4565	45XX class
	4410	44XX class		4545	45XX class		5531	4575 class		4568	45XX class
				4556	45XX class		5540	4575 class		4570	45XX class
1926	4400	44XX class		4561	45XX class					4598	4575 class
	4402	44XX class		4581	4575 class	1941	4410	44XX class		5502	4575 class
	4406	44XX class		4598	4575 class		4528	45XX class		5519	4575 class
	4410	44XX class		5502	4575 class		4531	45XX class		5531	4575 class
	4523	45XX class		5526	4575 class		4542	45XX class			
	4563	45XX class					4565	45XX class	1948	4503	45XX class
			1933	Records not available			5519	4575 class		4516	45XX class
1927	4400	44XX class					5525	4575 class		4526	45XX class
	4401	44XX class	1934	4400	44XX class		5531	4575 class		4529	45XX class
	4402	44XX class		4401	44XX class					4552	45XX class
	4405	44XX class		4405	44XX class	1942	4503	45XX class		4559	45XX class
	4410	44XX class		4406	44XX class		4512	45XX class		4565	45XX class
	4538	45XX class		4409	44XX class		4528	45XX class		4570	45XX class
	4578	4575 class		4523	45XX class		4542	45XX class		5519	4575 class
				4526	45XX class		4552	45XX class			
1928	4401	44XX class		4543	45XX class		4559	45XX class			
	4404	44XX class		4545	45XX class		5519	4575 class			
	4405	44XX class		4598	4575 class		5525	4575 class			
	4410	44XX class		5526	4575 class		5569	4575 class			
	4515	45XX class									
	4523	45XX class	1935	4400	44XX class	1943	4503	45XX class			
	4538	45XX class		4405	44XX class		4505	45XX class			
	4540	45XX class		4521	45XX class		4548	45XX class			
	4564	45XX class		4543	45XX class		4552	45XX class			
	4578	4575 class		4545	45XX class		4559	45XX class			
				4548	45XX class		4565	45XX class			
1929	4404	44XX class		4549	45XX class		4598	4575 class			
	4405	44XX class		4598	4575 class		5525	4575 class			
	4512	45XX class					5531	4575 class			
	4516	45XX class	1936	4410	44XX class						
	4523	45XX class		4521	45XX class	1944	4407	44XX class			
	4525	45XX class		4526	45XX class		4503	45XX class			
	4538	45XX class		4528	45XX class		4505	45XX class			
	4548	45XX class		4531	45XX class		4552	45XX class			
	4564	45XX class		4538	45XX class		4559	45XX class			
	4578	4575 class		4542	45XX class		4565	45XX class			
	4583	4575 class		4543	45XX class		4570	45XX class			
				4545	45XX class		4598	4575 class			
1930	4508	45XX class		4548	45XX class		5525	4575 class			
	4523	45XX class		4549	45XX class		5531	4575 class			
	4525	45XX class									
	4538	45XX class	1937	4410	44XX class	1945	4407	44XX class			
	4553	45XX class		4502	45XX class		4503	45XX class			
	4556	45XX class		4512	45XX class		4505	45XX class			
	4565	45XX class		4528	45XX class		4529	45XX class			
	4573	45XX class		4531	45XX class		4552	45XX class			
	4576	4575 class		4534	45XX class		4565	45XX class			
	4578	4575 class		4538	45XX class		4568	45XX class			
	4582	4575 class		4542	45XX class		4570	45XX class			
	5501	4575 class		4545	45XX class		4598	4575 class			
	5522	4575 class					5525	4575 class			

No. 4405 at Looe on 23rd May 1935. The new 'B set' coaches Nos. 6904/6 were only on the line for one season before they were replaced with older vehicles having 7ft wheelbase bogies. *H. C. Casserley*

was dieselised in 1958, some of the engines were dispersed to other sheds on the Western Region. No. 5572 subsequently appeared at Moorswater and remained on the line, still fitted with its auto gear, until the end of steam services in September 1961.

Around 1930 bogie carriages were introduced to replace the old four-wheeled coaches. There were two pairs of brake composite vehicles, identified in the carriage working programme as 'B sets', together with an additional vehicle as a 'spare' to strengthen the regular train at busy periods. During the early 1930s, wooden panelled vehicles of the 1890s were provided but in 1934 these were replaced with new vehicles. The *Railway Magazine* for that September reported that in mid-June two standard GWR corridor coaches, Nos. 5744 and 5748 (eight compartment thirds measuring 63ft 6in x 9ft), were tested over the Liskeard and Looe branch, with 2–6–2T No. 4513. The reporter speculated on the working of through coaches between Looe and other parts of the GWR system – and the possibility of a through portion to Looe from the 'Cornish Riviera Limited'. However, it seems that the test run was not a success for henceforth the appendix to the working timetable included the following note: 'Eight-wheel stock exceeding 63ft 6in by 9ft 5¾in must not work over the Looe branch'. Nevertheless, by November of 1934 two pairs of new steel-panelled brake composites arrived on the line to work the service. The new vehicles were specifically allocated to the branch and had the legend 'Looe Branch No. 1' and 'Looe Branch No. 2' painted

on the outer ends of each pair. At least one of the old wooden panelled brake composite vehicles was retained as a spare vehicle.

Perhaps through undue flange wear caused by their 9ft wheelbase bogies, the new vehicles remained for only one year, after which they were exchanged with similar vehicles from the Bristol area which, apart from being a few years older, built in 1929 and having radiused bow-ends, differed in being fitted with shorter 7ft wheelbase bogies.

There was apparently a problem with the sharp radius of curves in the yard at Liskeard because the appendix to the working timetable contained the following note: 'The connection between the Main line and the Looe line is not available for trains conveying passengers. Owing to the sharp curve, every care must be exercised in shunting movements over this connection'. For that reason the possibility of through running of coaches from the 'Cornish Riviera Limited' and other trains remained unfulfilled, and the appendix included the additional instruction 'Stock working on the Looe branch must be fitted with 7 feet wheelbase bogies'. The replacement vehicles arrived in November 1935 and from that date onwards similar coaches remained in use until the end of steam on the line.

Later a 'loose' brake composite was allocated to the line for strengthening purposes. This coach was built in 1937 and, being specially equipped with the required 7ft wheelbase bogies, had the painted instruction on the body side 'Return to Liskeard'. In the late 1930s two thirds were used and in the late 1950s main-line corridor stock was

This 1937-built Brake Composite coach, marked 'Return to Liskeard' on the lower body side, was photographed in the carriage siding at Liskeard during the 1950s.
Author's collection

sometimes used for strengthening, but, in accordance with the standing instructions, only vehicles with 7ft wheelbase bogies could be used.

In 1957, two 'B sets' were allocated to the line, set No. 54 working the 9.55 a.m. Liskeard to Looe and 10.55 a.m. Looe to Liskeard, and the second 'B set' working all the remaining branch services. Similar arrangements remained in place until the end of steam in 1961.

The first diesel multiple units sent to work on the branch from the commencement of the winter timetable in 1961 were 3-car sets built at Derby works in 1957 for suburban services. Later designated class 116, these ran from their depot at Plymouth at the start of each day's service and returned there at the close of service. By the mid-1960s, similar DMUs, built in 1959 by the Pressed Steel Company, were in use although, reflecting the amount of traffic available in the winter, they often ran as a two-car set with the centre coach removed. The Swindon-built cross-country DMUs could also be seen, again often working with the centre coach taken out of the formation.

Latterly a single car would often suffice, and similar units remain at work on the line at the time of writing. There was an attempt, in 1986, to introduce new stock to the line when Class 142 'Pacer' units were brought to Cornwall to work the remaining branch lines. Consisting of two four-wheeled vehicles with very long wheelbase, these units were doomed from the outset on the sharply-curved Looe branch. The flanges protested loudly on the sharp curves and they could be heard squealing down the valley long before they came into view. They lasted for one season only before being transferred away to West Yorkshire, and the by now old 'modernisation plan' DMUs returned to the line.

Goods services were worked by the North British-built 1,100 h.p. Bo-Bo D63XX class, later BR class 22, at first to Looe but, from 1963, to the clay dries at Moorswater only. From 1971, when the D63XX class was withdrawn, Sulzer Type 2, Class 25s, took over the freight working and these in turn were superseded by the English Electric Co-Co Class 37s which continue to run to and from Moorswater to the present day.

Although the Liskeard and Caradon company owned a number of wagons, they were primarily employed on mineral working between Caradon and Looe and would not have ventured onto the GWR. Indeed, when the Great Western took over the line in 1909, the L & C goods stock was in such poor condition and of such antiquated design that it was quickly disposed of. Goods traffic otherwise employed standard GWR and other companies' vehicles and there was nothing extraordinary about the wagons used.

As was the Great Western tradition on such lines, a goods brake van was specifically allocated to the Looe branch. In 1920, 'special brake van' No. 12022 was recorded in use on the branch. This was a standard GWR goods brake van fitted with side loading doors in the covered portion for the conveyance of small goods consignments and parcels. Originally employed on the Helston branch, by February 1923 it had been reallocated to Oswestry for working on the Abermule–Kerry branch. In the 1950s, 'standard' ex-GWR 20-ton goods brake van No. W68613 was allocated to the line branded 'Liskeard R.U. To Work Between Liskeard Looe & Menheniot', the initials R.U. indicating that the van was in 'restricted use'.

APPENDICES

LISKEARD AND LOOE BRANCH.

The speed of trains over the Branch not to exceed 25 miles per hour.
Single Line worked by Electric Train Token Liskeard to Looe.   Intermediate Crossing place Coombe Junction.

Down Trains.   Week Days.   Sundays.
Commencing June 5th, 1938.

Distance via Coombe Jct. Station.	STATIONS.	Ruling gradient 1 in	Time allowances for Ordinary Freight Trains (see page 2.)			B Pass. Q dep. A.M.	B Mixed § dep. A.M.		B Pass. dep. A.M.	B Pass. dep. A.M.	B Goods * dep. P.M.	B Pass. P dep.		B Pass. dep. P.M.		B Pass. dep. P.M.		B Pass. dep. P.M.		B Pass. dep. P.M.	B Pass. M dep. P.M.	B Pass. ¶ dep. P.M.	B Pass. dep. A.M.	B Pass. dep. A.M.	B Pass. dep. P.M.	B Pass. dep. P.M.	B Pass. dep. P.M.	B Pass. dep. P.M.
			Point to Point times. Mins.	Allow for stop. Mins.	Allow for start. Mins.																							
M. C.	Liskeard		—	—	1	5 20	7 25	..	9 0	11 20	12 15	1 30	..	3 5	..	4 45	..	5 48	..	7 30	9 5	8 45	10 40	12 5	2 0	4 5	7 35
— 37	Stop Board	273 F	1	2	1	P						P	....		....												
2 5	Coombe J.S.	35 F	5	1	1	—	7 36	..	9 9	11 29	12 28	1 39	..	3 14	..	4X54	..	5 57	..	7 39	9 14	8 54	10 49	12 14	2 9	4 14	7 44
3 64	St. Keyne	121 F	—	—	—	CR	7 40	..	9 13	11 33	A	1 43	....	3 18	..	4 58	..	6 1	..	7 43	9 18	8 58	10 53	12 18	2 13	4 18	7 48
5 9	Causeland	180 F	—	—	—	CR	—	..	9 17	11 37	—	1 47	....	3 22	..	5 2	..	6 5	..	7 47	9 22	9 2	10 57	12 22	2 17	4 22	7 52
6 39	Sandplace	160 F	11	1	1	CR	7 49	..	9 22	11 42	1 14	1 52	....	3 27	..	5 7	..	6 10	..	7 52	9 27	9 7	11 2	12 27	2 22	4 27	7 57
8 54	Looe ..	L	6	1	1	5 45	7 54	..	9 27	11 47	1 22	1 57	..	3 32	..	5 12	..	6 15	..	7 57	9 32	9 12	11 7	12 32	2 27	4 32	8 2

A Arrives Moorswater 12.32 p.m. and departs 12.47 p.m. for Looe.   M Saturdays only also December 24th, 1937, and April 14th, 1938.
Q Runs December 25th, 1937, April 15th, and Saturdays commencing June 4th, 1938.   * Engine depart Moorswater 11.45 a.m.   § Engine depart Moorswater 6.45 a.m.
¶ Engine depart Moorswater 8.20 a.m.

Up Trains.   Week Days.   Sundays.
Commences June 5th, 1938.

M.P. Mileage.	STATIONS.	Ruling gradient 1 in	Time allowances for Ordinary Freight Trains (see page 2.)			D Empty Q dep. A.M.	B Pass. dep. A.M.		B Pass. dep. A.M.	B Passr. dep. P.M.	B Pass. dep. P.M.	B Goods ¶ dep.		B Passr. dep. P.M.	B RR Cattle last Mon in month. dep. P.M.	B Pass. dep. P.M.		B Passr. dep. P.M.	B Pass. dep. P.M.	B Passr. M dep. P.M.	B Pass. dep. A.M.	B Pass. dep. A.M.	B Pass. dep. P.M.	B Pass. dep. P.M.	B Pass. dep. P.M.	B Pass. dep. P.M.
			Point to Point times. Mins.	Allow for stop. Mins.	Allow for start. Mins.																					
M. C.	Looe		—	—	1	6 25	8 15	..	9 50	12 20	2 20	2 40	..	4 0	4 30	5 20	..	6 40	8 15	9 45	9 55	11 25	1 15	3 15	4 45	8 20
2 28	Sandplace	L	6	1	1	—	8 21	..	9 56	12 26	2 26	—	..	4 6	—	—	..	6 46	8 20	9 51	10 1	11 31	1 21	3 21	6 46	8 26
3 58	Causeland	160 R	4	1	1	—	8 25	...	10 0	12 30	2 30	—	..	4 10	—	—	..	6 50	8 25	9 55	10 5	11 35	1 25	3 25	6 50	8 30
5 3	St. Keyne	180 R	4	1	1	—	8 29	...	10 4	12 34	2 34	—	..	4 14	—	—	..	6 54	8 29	9 59	10 9	11 39	1 29	3 29	6 54	8 34
6 62	Coombe J.S.	121 R	5	1	1	6 43	8 36	..	10 11	12 41	2 41	3 25	..	4 21	X5 10	CS	..	7 1	8 35	10 3	10 16	11 46	1 36	3 36	7 1	8 41
8 66	Liskeard ...	35 R	9	1		6 50	8 43	..	10 18	12 48	2 48	3 36	..	4 28	5 20	5 43	..	7 8	8Z43	10Y15	10 23	11 53	1 43	3 43	7 8	8T48

The Guard issues Tickets intermediately at Sandplace, Causeland, St. Keyne and Coombe Junction.

M Saturdays only, also December 24th, 1937, and April 14th, 1938.   Q Runs December 25th, 1937, April 15th and Saturdays commencing June 4th, 1938.   T Light Engine to Moorswater at 9.0 p.m.   Y Light Engine to Moorswater 10.20 p.m.   Z Light Engine to Moorswater 8.50 p.m. SX   ¶ Moorswater arrive 3.5 p.m., depart 3.20 p.m.

Taken from GWR Service Timetable for 27th September 1937 to 3rd July 1938.

LISKEARD AND LOOE.

THE SPEED OF TRAINS OVER THE BRANCH NOT TO EXCEED 25 MILES PER HOUR.
Single Line worked by Electric Train Token Liskeard to Looe.   Intermediate Crossing Place Coombe Junction.

Down Trains.   Week Days only.

Distance via Coombe Junction Station.	STATIONS.	Ruling gradient 1 in	Time Allowances for Ordinary Freight Trains. See page 5.			G Engine. SX dep. a.m.	B Pass. SO dep. a.m.	B Pass. SO dep. a.m.	B Mixed § dep. a.m.	G Engine SO June 19th to Sept. 25th (inc.). dep. a.m.	B Pass. SO dep. a.m.	B Pass. SX dep. a.m.	B Passenger. arr. dep. a.m. a.m.	B Pass. SO dep. a.m.	K Freight. H arr. dep. a.m.	B Pass. dep. p.m.	B Pass. dep. p.m.	B Pass. dep. p.m.	B Pass. dep. p.m.
			Point to Point times. Mins.	Allow for Stop. Mins.	Allow for Start. Mins.		N						U						
M. C.	LISKEARD	—	—	—	1	4 40	6 0	7 15		8 55	V	11 23		1 25	2 55	4 40	5 55	7 45
— 37	Stop Board	60 F	1	2	1			P					P					
2 5	Coombe Junction	34 F	5	1	1	4|45¼	CS	CS	7 24	8 49	9 4	10 9X	10 13	11 32 12 18A 12 54	1 34	3 4	4 49	6 4	7 54
3 64	St. Keyne	121 F							7 28		8 53	9 8	— 10 17	11 36		1 38	3 8	4 53	6 8	7 58
5 9	Causeland	103 F	1	1	1				7 32		8 57	9 12	— 10 21	11 40		1 42	3 12	4 57	6 12	8 2
6 39	Sandplace	160 F	11	1	1		5 5	6 25	7 37		9 2	9 17	— 10 25	11 45	1 5 1 10	1 47	3 17	5 2	6 17	8 7
8 51	LOOE	107 F	6	1		5|| 0			7 42	8||40	9 7	9 22	10 30	11 50	1 18	1 52	3 22	5 7	6 22	8 12

A—Arrive Moorswater 12.17 p.m. and depart 12.50 p.m. for Coombe Junction.   H—On Saturdays not to be held after 1.35 p.m. for 9.40 a.m. Bristol (due Liskeard 1.20 p.m.).   N—Engine depart Moorswater 4||15 a.m.   U—May be held until 11.42 a.m. for 11.35 p.m. Liverpool to Penzance (or 10.43 a.m. North Road of preceding).   V—Engine depart Moorswater 9.30 a.m.!   §—Not to convey Freight traffic on Saturdays.   ‡—Moorswater departure.

Up Trains.   Week Days only.

M.P. Mileage. (From Looe Quay.)	STATIONS.	Ruling gradient 1 in	Time Allowances for Ordinary Freight Trains. See page 55.			B Workmen. dep. a.m.	B Pass. SO dep. a.m.	B Pass. SO dep. a.m.	B Pass. SX dep. a.m.	B Pass. SO June 19th to Sept. 25th (inc.). dep. a.m.	B Passenger. arr. dep. a.m. a.m.	B Pass. dep. a.m.	K Freight. SO arr. dep. a.m. a.m.	B Pass. dep. p.m.	B Pass. dep. p.m.	B Pass. dep. p.m.	B Passenger. arr. dep. p.m. p.m.
			Point to Point times. Mins.	Allow for Stop. Mins.	Allow for Start. Mins.												
M. C.	LOOE	—	—	—	1	5 20	6 40	8 15	9 20		9 40 10 45	12 20	2 10	2 30	4 6 5 20	6 40		8 30
2 28	Sandplace	107 F	6	1	1	5 26	8 1	8 21	—		9 46 10 51	12 26	—		4 6	6 46	—	8 36
3 58	Causeland	160 R	4	1	1	5 30	8 5	8 25	—		9 50 10 55	12 30	—		4 10	6 50	—	8 40
5 3	St. Keyne	103 R	4	1	1	5 34	8 9	8 29	—		9 54 10 59	12 34	—		4 14	6 54	—	8 44
6 62	Coombe Junction	121 R	5	1	1	5 41	CS	8 36	CS	9 58X	10 6 11 6	12 41	CS	2 51 3 15	4 21	CS	—	8 51
8 67	LISKEARD	34 R	9	1		5 48	7 6	8X23	8 43	10 17	11 13	12 48	12 48	4 28	5 46	7 8	8 58	Z

Y—Not advertised to connect into 11.50 p.m. Paddington to Penzance.   Z—Light Engine to Moorswater 9.5 p.m.   ¶—Moorswater arrive 2.55 p.m., depart 3.10 p.m.
The Guard issues tickets intermediately at Sandplace, Causeland, St. Keyne and Coombe Junction.

Taken from GWR Service Timetable for 31st May 1948.

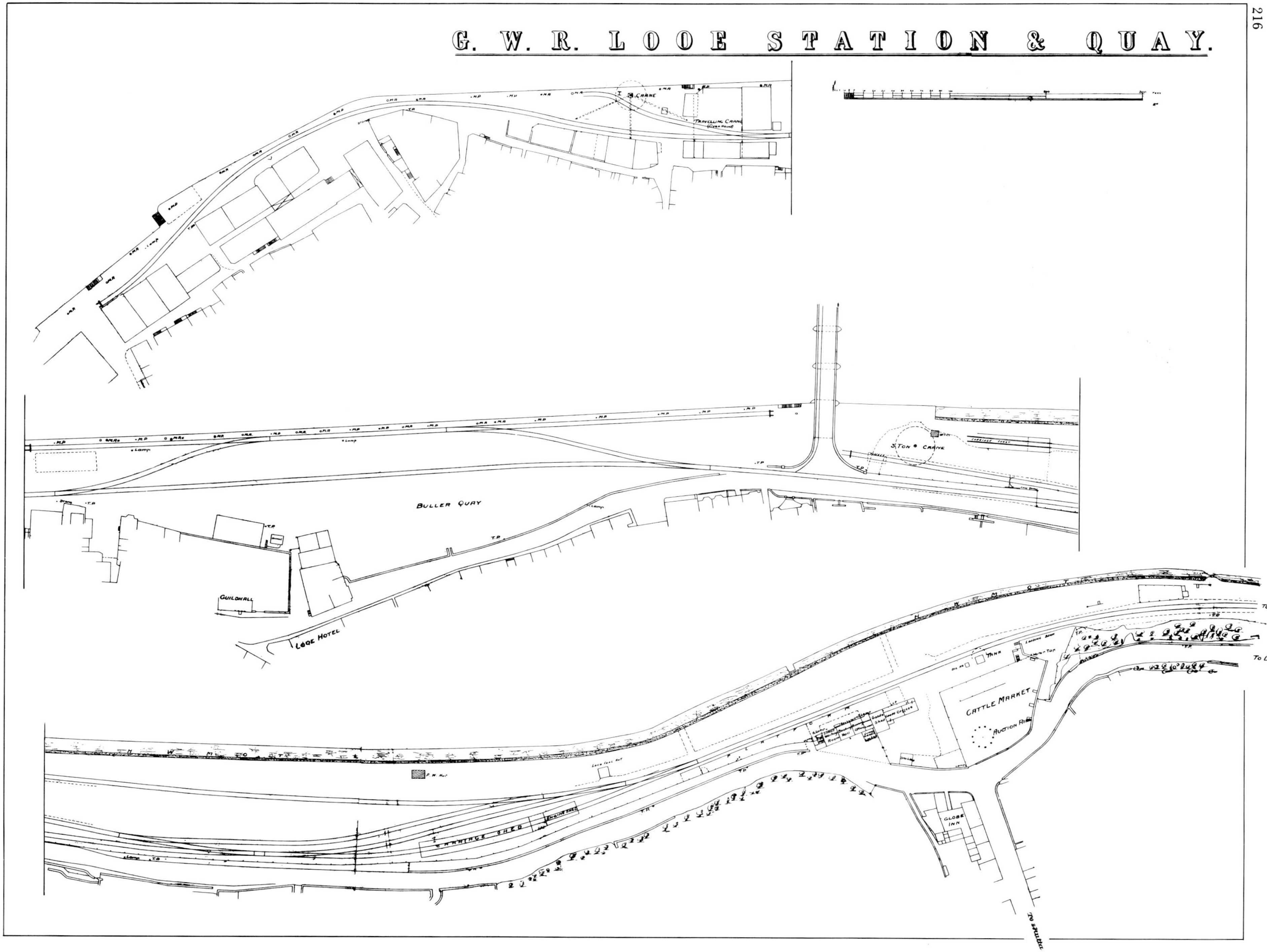

G. W. R. LOOE STATION & QUAY.

BULLER QUAY

LOOE HOTEL

GUILDHALL

CATTLE MARKET

AUCTION RM.

GLOBE INN

To Liskeard

To Liskeard

To Hatha

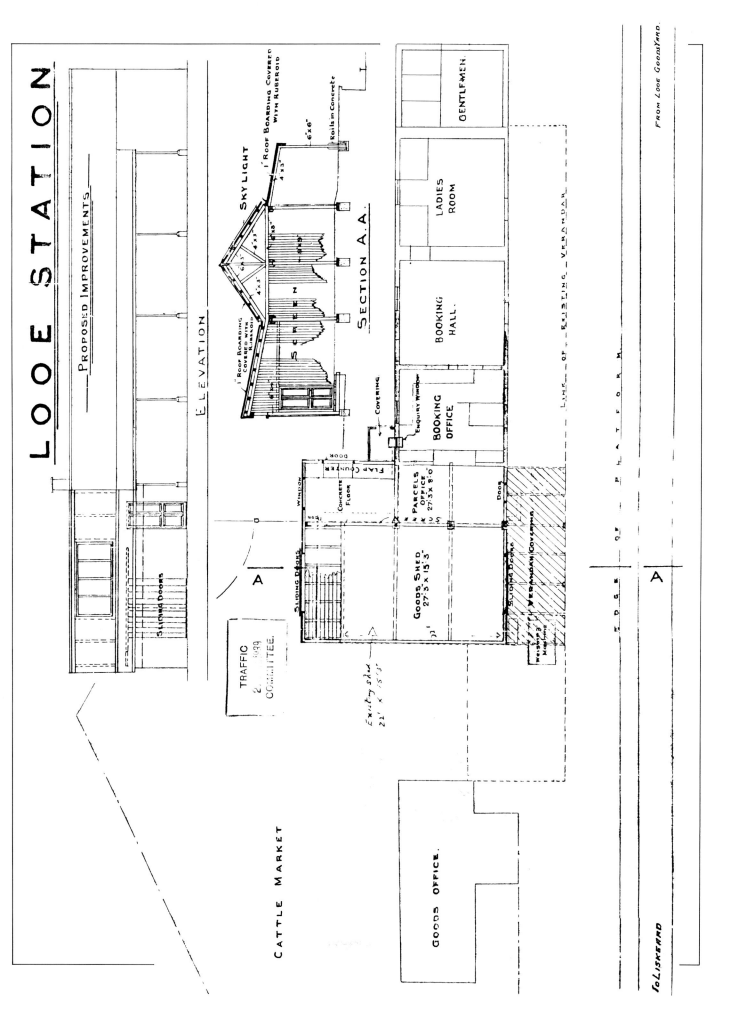

LOOE STATION

PROPOSED IMPROVEMENTS

ELEVATION

SECTION A.A.

SkyLight

1" Roof Boarding Covered with Ruberoid

6"×6"

Rails in Concrete

4"×3"

4"×3"

4"×3"

1" Roof Boarding Covered with Ruberoid

SCREEN

Sliding Doors

CATTLE MARKET

TRAFFIC
2. 1939.
COMMITTEE.

A

A

Existing shed
21' × 15'3"

Sliding Doors

DOOR

Window

Concrete Floor

Goods Shed
27'3" × 15'3"

Covering

FLAP COUNTER

Enquiry Window

BOOKING OFFICE

PARCELS OFFICE
27'3" × 8'0"

Door

Door

Weighing Machine

Verandah Covering

Sliding Doors

GENTLEMEN.

LADIES ROOM

BOOKING HALL.

LINE OF EXISTING VERANDAH

EDGE OF PLATFORM

GOODS OFFICE.

GOODS OFFICE.

FROM LOOE GOODS YARD.

TO LISKEARD

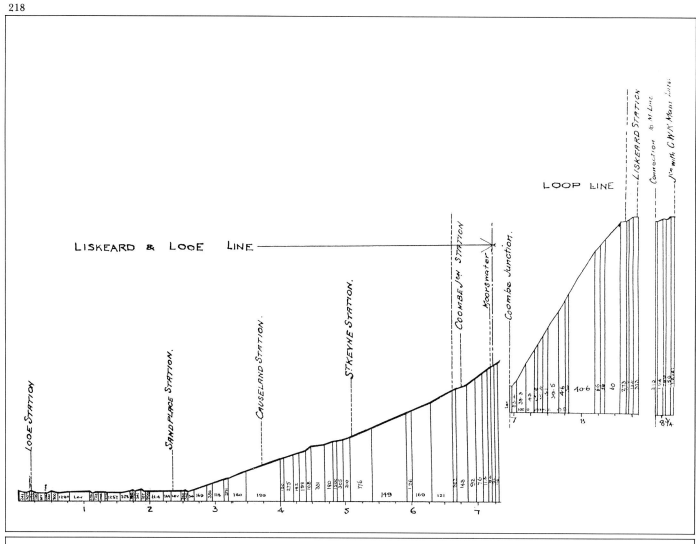

LISKEARD & LOOE LINE

LOOP LINE

LOOE STATION

SAND PLACE STATION.

CAUSELAND STATION.

ST. KEYNE STATION.

COOMBE JCN STATION.

Moorswater.

Coombe Junction.

LISKEARD STATION.

Connection to N! Line.

Jcn with G.W.R. Main Line.

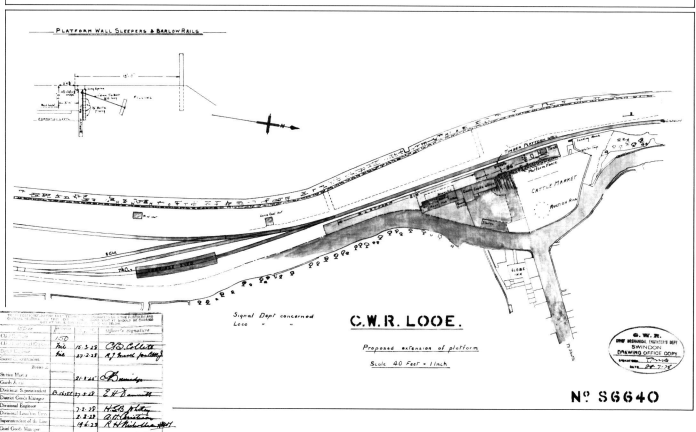

PLATFORM WALL SLEEPERS & BARLOW RAILS

CATTLE MARKET

AUCTION RING

GLOBE INN

Signal Dept concerned
Loco " "

C.W.R. LOOE.

Proposed extension of platform

Scale 40 Feet = 1 Inch

Nº S6640